RELATIONSHIP, RESPONSIBILITY, AND REGULATION

RELATIONSHIP

RESPONSIBILITY  AND

REGULATION

TRAUMA-INVESTED PRACTICES FOR FOSTERING RESILIENT LEARNERS

Kristin Van Marter Souers
with Pete Hall

ASCD | ALEXANDRIA, VA USA

1703 N. Beauregard St. • Alexandria, VA 22311-1714 USA
Phone: 800-933-2723 or 703-578-9600 • Fax: 703-575-5400
Website: www.ascd.org • E-mail: member@ascd.org
Author guidelines: www.ascd.org/write

Deborah S. Delisle, *Executive Director;* Stefani Roth, *Publisher;* Genny Ostertag, *Director, Content Acquisitions;* Julie Houtz, *Director, Book Editing & Production;* Miriam Calderone, *Editor;* Judi Connelly, *Associate Art Director;* Donald Ely, *Senior Graphic Designer;* Circle Graphics, *Typesetter;* Mike Kalyan, *Director, Production Services;* Shajuan Martin, *E-Publishing Specialist*

PAPERBACK ISBN: 978-1-4166-2685-5   ASCD product #119027   n12/18
PDF E-BOOK ISBN: 978-1-4166-2687-9; see Books in Print for other formats.
Quantity discounts are available: e-mail programteam@ascd.org or call 800-933-2723, ext. 5773, or 703-575-5773. For desk copies, go to www.ascd.org/deskcopy.

Library of Congress Cataloging-in-Publication Data is available for this title.
LCCN: 2018048684

27 26 25 24 23 22 21 20 19   2 3 4 5 6 7 8 9 10 11 12

I want to dedicate this book to my mom. Thank you for being such a positive influence in my life. Your intelligence, strength, loyalty, and tenacity have taught me so much. I love you so very much.
—*Kristin Van Marter Souers*

This book is for all our fellow travelers. Wherever you are in the journey, may you safely and confidently step forward.
—*Pete Hall*

RELATIONSHIP, RESPONSIBILITY, AND REGULATION

··

Trauma-Invested Practices for Fostering Resilient Learners

Acknowledgments

This is my favorite part of the book because it is my chance to say thank you! I remain humbled and overwhelmed by the responses Pete and I have received since the publication of *Fostering Resilient Learners*. I am grateful every day for the work you do on behalf of children and families. You are needed more than ever to provide children with a safe and predictable environment, and you are truly making a difference. (That said, make sure to take care of yourself, too!)

I also want to thank Genny and Miriam at ASCD for their amazing partnership and faith in us to write this second book. They are true joys to work with, and I feel so lucky to have them. I am also grateful to Donald for listening to our vision for the book cover and designing yet another great visual. His talents are incredible!

A special thanks to my partner in writing and presenting, Pete Hall. I never imagined our work together would lead to this, and I am grateful every day that it did. Thank you for pushing me to be my best person. Your humor and positive attitude are so inspiring! Thank you, my friend—thank you!

I also want to thank the many people out there who have taken the risk to be vulnerable in this work. I am so grateful for your courage and your willingness to deeply explore trauma-invested work. I feel so blessed to have worked with so many of you and humbled by your honesty and your stories. Thank you for your courage and your commitment. The world is a better place because of you!

I feel lucky to have so many valuable people in my life. I am surrounded by such support. For this book, I want to give a special shoutout to the strong women in my life. Thank you to all of you for your amazing work and love. I am better because of you!

I want to especially acknowledge my mom, Molly; my sister, Stephanie; and my daughter, Katlynn. These women are truly talented, amazing, and incredible people. I can't imagine my life without them, and I am grateful for them every day. They have shown me the power of strength and courage. Throughout all the hardships and challenges they have experienced, they have managed to stay true to themselves and not waver. Their perseverance is so admirable. They also taught me to have hope again. During one of my tougher times, my sister gave me a sign with a powerful message. That sign still sits in my dining room as a friendly reminder for me to trust. These amazing women gave me permission to believe in myself and to commit to doing what I am passionate about without fear—to just take that leap, and to feel love again.

This is my wish for you, my brave readers: to remember to have hope and not let fear drive your bus. In these times, we need to remember to be kind to one another and to believe in the goodness of humans. We need to remember to trust. In the words of my amazing sister's message to me: "Not to spoil the ending, but everything is going to be OK."

Peace,
Kristin

Preface

I write books because educators have asked me to. Pete encouraged me to write my first book, *Fostering Resilient Learners,* and I am so grateful that it resonated with so many people. In that book, my goal was to highlight approaches for the adult in creating a trauma-sensitive learning environment that were accessible and worth the time invested. Time is valuable, and there's never enough of it. Whenever I train and consult, I want attendees to walk away saying, "Now that was a good use of my time!" When you're finished with the last paragraph in the last chapter of this book, I hope you say the same thing. I also want you to walk away feeling challenged, energized, and equipped with ideas for how best to support yourself, your team, and your students and families.

I am blessed to have been able to write both my books near the ocean. Water is my happy place. I love to be able to write, walk, think, write, run, challenge myself, and write again. I always come away from these experiences mindful of where I have let my own work-life balance go and appreciative of the many blessings I have in life. I think we can all benefit from giving ourselves more time to reflect—to feel gratitude and appreciation, to give ourselves and others more grace, and to contemplate how we can influence the world in more positive ways. I want us to remember to be kind. Life is hard and messy, and we could all use a little more kindness in our world. So please remember to treat yourself and others with kindness. A smile or a high-five can go a long way! I truly hope you enjoy this book. Thank you for sharing your time with me.

Kristin Van Marter Souers, Spokane, Washington, January 2018

I've been a professional educator for more than 20 years, 14 of which I spent as a school administrator and the last 4 as a professional development agent working with schools and districts across the globe—an incredible vantage point from which to see the education opera play out in its totality. From age 5 (and younger) to age 18 (and beyond), we run our students through a gauntlet and expect them to become competent, educated, responsible, thoughtful citizens when they're done. In case y'all haven't noticed, it doesn't always work out that way.

One of the primary culprits? Stuff. *Stuff* happens. As educators and as professionals in the caregiving fields, it's our responsibility to reduce the impact that *stuff* has on our kids. We can't stop the not-OK from happening, Kristin tells us, but we can mitigate its negative effects. And we can most definitely create an environment that is safe, predictable, and consistent so our young people can be OK with their not-OK.

Another factor impeding our success rate? Ourselves. It may make us uncomfortable to admit this, but we often act in ways that run contrary to our stated goals. We enact rigid policies that ignore the uniqueness of every child and every circumstance, we create procedures that are unrealistic and driven by politics and fear rather than by students' needs and high-quality research, and we implement practices that result in frustration and burnout at both the educator and educatee levels.

We can do better.

In partnering with Kristin a decade ago, I realized what a tremendous message she shares. The mindsets she espouses aren't revolutionary, but they can have revolutionary effects. The strategies she's collected are tried and true. I've personally seen them work in two schools where

I was principal, when I brought in Kristin to work with the staff and school community. I witnessed the transformation and growth along the trauma-savvy spectrum (which you'll read more about in Chapter 1). I've felt the shifts. And I've seen the results.

Partnering with Kristin to write *Fostering Resilient Learners* was an easy decision. If we can expand the audience and distribute her message to educators nationwide—heck, worldwide—let's do it. Through our two books, and through presentations and workshops and consulting support at the national, state, and local levels, we are living that mission.

In our quest to build your capacity, we now invite you to turn your lens toward the most precious element of your professional responsibilities: your students.

Pete Hall, Coeur d'Alene, Idaho, January 2018

Introduction

Create a safe nest for students so that they learn and thrive and, when they eventually fly, they soar.

The above sentence is my new mission for schools. It's not that unreasonable or outside the realm of possibility, is it? As educators, we have an obligation to provide an opportunity for all students—every single one of them—to learn and grow and become the best they can be. I want every adult in education to see all kids (and one another) as competent, special, and *awesome*.

Unfortunately, the demands on educators and others in the helping and caregiving professions are ridiculously high. Many of us would agree that our societal systems are less than ideal; indeed, some might argue that they're downright broken. Although they are well-intentioned, these systems—education, mental health, medical, family services, legal, and others—are not equipped with the resources or the vision and permission to truly achieve what is needed. No matter which of these fields you're in, I'm betting your job, while hopefully rewarding, is also difficult and challenging and, at times, overwhelming. Your hard work may go underappreciated and unacknowledged. That can get old fast.

I am here to tell you that we can change that. We may not be able to change systems overnight, but we can make a difference every day in the lives of those we serve.

This Book Is for You

As a mental health provider, I learned early in my career that there just weren't enough resources in place to meet the need for services. For that reason, I decided to partner with education. School is the one place kids are guaranteed to go, and I knew, based on the prevalence of childhood trauma, that many students were falling through the cracks and being misunderstood. I knew educators were not equipped with the knowledge or the skill set to truly understand how disruptive trauma could be to the learning process. So, I made it my mission to connect with education professionals and help them provide trauma-sensitive environments that would enhance student learning. It is through that training and outreach that I met Pete.

Since the publication of *Fostering Resilient Learners* in 2016, Pete and I have received a tremendous response from our readers. I am so humbled. When I set out to write that book, I had no idea that recording the lessons I've learned, the information I've gathered, and the strategies I've employed during the last two decades would have such a profound effect on my colleagues and partners in the field. It has been amazing, validating, and, honestly, quite overwhelming! We have received personal notes and feedback from thousands of educators and caregiving professionals from around the world, sharing the impact our book has had.

During the last two years, Pete and I have been fortunate to be able to work with school districts, provide consulting services to scores of educator teams, and speak at education and other professional conferences throughout the United States. There is such a need for professional development, continued learning, and mindset shifting—and we are committed to helping however we can. Together, we work with systems dedicated to helping humans in positive, healthy ways.

Now, based on reader requests—or should I say reader demands—I bring you this new guide to providing trauma-invested practices for your students and families. This book is for students, parents, education professionals, mental health providers, coaches, support staff, administrators, and anyone else who has a passion for helping humans.

As you travel on this journey with me, I will challenge you as a professional to enhance your own understanding of your beliefs, your mission, your perspective, and the influence you have on the settings in which you work. I look at the importance of self-care and maintaining a healthy work-life balance, and I weave examples and stories throughout the text to give you insights into the many challenges we all face and ways to overcome them.

The Focus of This Book

In *Fostering Resilient Learners*, Pete and I focused solely on the professional—on enhancing your self-awareness to help you be the best you can be for your students and families. Our thesis was simple: you've got to build awareness of the issues and take care of yourself in order to help others. This emphasis was meant to help you see that although you cannot stop trauma from happening, you can create a setting that is safe for students.

We refer to this setting as a *positive learning environment:* one that addresses the whole child so that teaching and learning can flourish.

But a question we hear time and time again from professionals is this: "OK, I've learned about adverse childhood experiences. I believe in each of my kids. I understand my mission, and I can keep myself grounded amid chaos. Now what do I do about the student in my classroom who is having an incredibly difficult time, right now, right in front of me? I've got strategies to help *me*, but how can I help this child?"

Does this ring true for you? If so, you're in the right place. This book will challenge your beliefs and inspire deeper and different ways of thinking about your roles in teaching, youth development, and situations involving students. Pete and I believe the tenets of ASCD's whole child approach are five critical pieces of the puzzle that helps kids to learn, grow, and develop successfully. By providing environments where kids and adults are *healthy, safe, engaged, supported,* and *challenged,* we can meet our mission to help kids soar. Without these five components, we'll remain grounded, confined, and unfulfilled—as professionals, as students, as educators, and as human beings.

We all know the original three *R*s: reading, 'riting, and 'rithmetic. Now, with a trauma-informed lens, we are going to look at three new *R*s: relationship, responsibility, and regulation. These overarching ideas shape the positive learning environments we are establishing. They enhance the focus on the whole child. Student success—by whatever metric we use to define it—is going to be determined by the degree to which we can infuse these three components into the day-to-day operation of our classrooms, learning spaces, offices, and schools.

In the chapters that follow, I talk about the value of each of the new three *R*s and provide strategies to support your students and families. In actual scenarios provided by educators, I identify a student's unmet needs; examine the situation from each of five perspectives (student, parent/caregiver, teacher, support staff, and leader); and suggest interventions to support the student. Then I offer opportunities for reflection and pose guiding questions that allow you to dive deeper into your own thinking, actions, and approaches with all the stakeholders in each young person's life.

As in our first book, Pete supports and augments the findings and practices I share with timely insights from the school perspective. His "Pete's Practice" sections are woven into every chapter and help bring the strategies to life.

Although *Fostering Resilient Learners* (Souers & Hall, 2016) is not a prerequisite, Pete and I highly recommend reading it before embarking on this book, as it provides a thorough grounding in childhood trauma and its prevalence and lays a solid foundation for the strategies offered here. That said, in this book I do define key concepts and terms introduced in my first book so that you won't be lost if this is new territory. Having a knowledge base in this topic will be helpful. We in education tend to jump into strategies and try to find the fastest route to success. When we truly commit to a trauma-invested practice, however, our own self-awareness and knowledge of student needs are crucial to designing effective interventions.

As I explained in *Fostering Resilient Learners*, it is important to acknowledge five fundamental truths:

1. Trauma is real.
2. Trauma is prevalent. In fact, it is likely much more common than we care to admit.
3. Trauma is toxic to the brain and can affect development and learning in a multitude of ways.
4. In our schools, we need to be prepared to support students who have experienced trauma, even if we don't know exactly who they are.
5. Children are resilient, and within positive learning environments they can grow, learn, and succeed. (pp. 10–11)

As an educator, you can be the change agent for children and families. You have a unique opportunity to influence their lives, their attitudes, and their futures. And because this is so, *so* important, I want to do what I can to support you in fostering your own health and well-being, so you can be present, safe, and empowering to those you serve. It is my goal to equip you with the knowledge, awareness, and skills to support student success.

All students deserve an education, but to learn, they need to feel safe. You can provide that safe place for them.

PART

1

Part 1: Building the Nest

Culture of safety.
Systems of meaning.
Need versus behavior.

In Part 1, I emphasize the importance of establishing an environment in which our students can be OK with their not-OK. This, my friends, is the nest. Remember our new mission? *Create a safe nest for students so that they learn and thrive and, when they eventually fly, they soar.* This is our responsibility, it's within our sphere of influence, and it's essential for our students to experience success.

Just as we must till the soil and prepare the environment before our garden yields a healthy crop, so too must we tend to our learning environment. The first step is to create a culture of safety, which I'll explain in more detail in Chapter 1. For now, suffice it to say that it's an environment in which all feel valued and important, where we understand our students and see their potential. This environment extends beyond the learning locations where students find themselves; indeed, a safe and trusting professional environment that allows adults to work together and lean on one another in a healthy way is essential for us to do effective work with our students.

A big part of creating that culture of safety is examining our beliefs about our students and why they do what they do. That's right: we're going to look at *behaviors*. Student behaviors, in particular.

Misbehaviors, to be sure. They captivate our attention, they generate inner tumult, they wreak havoc on our lesson plans, they confound us. When we can make sense of the factors that influence student behaviors, we can approach *behavior management* (as opposed to classroom management) with much more utility, open-mindedness, and confidence.

That said, this is not a behavior management book. What I'm asking you to do is to dive much deeper than that. The elements you're going to explore include your assumptions about students, your thinking about student behaviors, various ways to employ empathy, and the unmet needs that drive student behaviors. It's not about "good versus bad" or even "appropriate versus inappropriate"; it's more about asking, "Why?"

As you roll up your sleeves, dig in, and unwrap the ideas I propose in the following chapters, there are a few things I want to emphasize:

1. The ideas and lenses I share are intended to truly challenge your thinking. I will be honest: there may be times when you are triggered and even feel some heated emotions. Pete and I are at peace with that, because it means you are really challenging yourself and your belief sets. Truly self-reflective practice is not easy, and facing the necessity to change our own thinking and practices can feel overwhelming.

2. Speaking of change, I love this one of Pete's many handy mantras: "Change is a prerequisite of improvement." Sometimes change is necessary, and the outcome we experience because of our courage to do what is right is more than worth the energy we put into making that change happen. The more we challenge and understand ourselves, the more self-aware we become. So, if this section challenges your thinking and causes you to pause and wonder about your need for change, trust me: that could be a really good thing.

3. Because the following three chapters are so immersed with ideas, we really challenge you to read through these chapters carefully and give yourself time for deep reflection. It is a lot of information to absorb. Give yourself permission to step away, journal some thoughts, and engage in dialogue with a trusted companion.

Have you ever watched a bird build a nest? Marveled at the systematic, relentless way each piece is nestled in with the others? Admired the dedication and love that motivate that investment of time, energy, and care? Appreciated the selfless passion for creating an environment that will foster resilient little chicks, even though the chicks might not even be there yet? Well, that bird is you. You can do this—and for your students' sake, you must, because this culture of safety is far too important to leave to chance, to leave to someone else, or to leave off entirely.

At the risk of repeating myself, I commend you on taking this journey to trauma-invested practice. Know that Pete and I will be with you along the way.

1

A Culture of Safety

When we explore the idea of trauma-sensitive practices, our purpose is to create an environment where it is safe for students to grow, to develop, to exist, and to learn. Pete and I refer to this as a positive learning environment, or "the nest" from the mission statement I shared in the Introduction. For those of us in education, this notion of "safety first" shouldn't be surprising. More than 70 years ago, Abraham Maslow (1943) introduced his hierarchy of needs (see Figure 1.1), which explained that beyond the basic physiological needs we have as human beings, safety is the essential external factor influencing our happiness, success, and very survival.

In this context, safety refers to two big ideas: physical safety and emotional safety. The reality is, if we don't feel safe, we can't lead, parent, teach, partner, or learn effectively. Our need to feel safe supersedes everything else.

Let's examine the level of safety that exists in our communities, our districts, our school buildings, and our classrooms. Currently, our

FIGURE 1.1
Maslow's Hierarchy of Needs

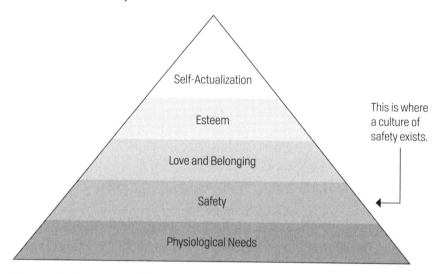

Source: From "A Theory of Human Motivation," by A. H. Maslow, 1943, *Psychological Review, 50*(4), pp. 370–396.

feelings of fear about our safety are heightened. We have experienced multiple events in our schools and communities that compromise our sense of trust. School shootings, acts of random violence, hate crimes, and other highly publicized and dangerous experiences can leave us feeling doubtful and concerned about our safety and that of our students.

The possibility that something "bad" will happen feels real, and many education professionals are doubting their capacity to make the right choices should a danger arise. Schools now run active-shooter drills in addition to fire drills, evacuation protocols, and earthquake preparedness—procedures intended to help us prepare for the worst. Although the odds are low that such an event will occur, those drills and policies are put in place for a reason. They were created because children and adults were murdered in schools, and we owe it to those victims to do whatever we can, whenever we can, to ensure the safety of all our students and to prevent further harm.

Safety goes beyond that extreme physical threat; it applies in a multitude of other areas as well. Let's explore what physical and emotional safety look like for ourselves and for our students.

Physical Safety

Adults. We have a need to feel that we are safe within the contexts of our settings. We should be able to walk through our doors and commence our work feeling confident that we can do our jobs safely. Many things can negatively affect our sense of physical safety, such as a student who uses aggression to regulate his or her emotions, a parent who threatens physical harm to protect his or her child, a building where the environment poses health risks, a community with adverse weather conditions, people who come to school with viruses and illnesses that compromise our own health, or the simple fatigue and lack of sleep associated with the stress of our roles.

Students. Our students also need to feel safe in their communities, buildings, and classroom settings. They need to know that school is a safe place where people care about their well-being. School should present an opportunity for them to walk through the doors and know that no harm will come to them while they are there. Many things can negatively affect a student's sense of physical safety, such as threat of physical harm from another student; a disruptive text message or Snapchat sent between classes; walking to and from school in a neighborhood riddled with crime and violence; having basic physical needs unmet and feeling tired, hungry, or cold; fighting illness and having to go to school anyway; poor classroom conditions; living in a community where weather poses a threat to safety; or living with abuse and feeling the repercussions of those experiences every day.

Emotional Safety

Adults. Working in an emotionally safe environment is critical to growth, success, and the cultivation of effective teaching and learning practices. We must feel safe enough to be vulnerable with our administrators and colleagues so that we can come forward to ask for support when we need it and access resources without fear of judgment or retaliation. When we are emotionally safe, we trust our leadership and our team to operate with the best interests of everyone in mind. Many things can negatively affect our ability to feel emotionally safe, including conflict with a coworker, toxic work environments that breed gossip and a deficit focus, lack of strong leadership, negative public perception and media coverage, hypercritical parents and caregivers, feelings of isolation and exhaustion, inability to feel safe asking for help, or feelings of failure or low self-efficacy in the job.

Students. Our students need to know that we, the adults in the building, see each one of them as valued, capable, and awesome. In a safe setting, they know that their mission is to learn and be successful. They can be vulnerable and ask for help without fear of judgment or criticism; they feel safe among their peers and treat one another with kindness; they are invested in the team, not just themselves; and they are committed to success. Many things can negatively affect a student's ability to feel emotionally safe, such as an adult who doesn't understand him or her, others' belief systems that portray and view that student in a negative light, students at school who use abusive or bullying behavior, inability to understand the dominant language of the school or community, being misunderstood by others because of cultural differences, or lacking the skills and confidence to come forward and safely seek support.

We all need to feel safe, both physically and emotionally. Without it, learning simply cannot happen. When you reflect on your work environment, how does this sense of safety apply to it?

Pete's Practice

As a school principal, I was hired to take over a school that had a significant history of—and reputation for—violence. There were reports of fights almost daily, and many students used physical aggression to settle their conflicts. When we dug deeper, my leadership team uncovered an ugly truth: the emotional safety of the adults and students was absent, so individuals within the building were always "on edge." And when we're at a heightened sense of alert, we biologically turn to flight-fight-freeze responses. Keep in mind that we all— cross-culturally and universally—choose flight first when sensing or experiencing threat. We choose to fight only when we don't see flight as an option. Many of our students at school face situations where simply leaving is not an option. We often see them access their fight response when in states of stress in an attempt to self-regulate.

Bringing Kristin into the building to help us learn trauma-sensitive strategies and to build trust within the ranks was an essential part of our overall plan to strengthen the collaborative, interdependent culture of the adults in the building. Once this took hold and we started to lean on one another, get some structures and policies squared away, and reinforce our mission and guiding values, our emotional safety metric skyrocketed. As a result, the tenor of the building shifted. The classrooms, hallways, and public areas became more peaceful, calmer, and safer. The fighting decreased, and the business of teaching and learning resumed.

Many factors were at play in this transformation, and I don't want to oversimplify the process. However, one key learning for us was that we couldn't solve the problem (lack of physical safety) solely by addressing the issue staring us in the face (kids fighting). We had to dig deeper and uncover the conditions that were contributing to that outcome (adults' lack of emotionally safety). It was surprising and incredibly enlightening to arrive at that conclusion.

Assumptions and Safety

As Pete's story illustrates, we need to be careful about how assumptions can affect safety. We often use assumptions to help us manage or make sense of a situation. We use them to enhance our understanding of something or affirm our belief sets about an event or a person. When we have only a piece of the puzzle, we tend to make assumptions based on past experiences and background information to fill in the gaps. Could be helpful, right? Well, you know what they say about assumptions: when you assume, you run the risk of making an *ass* out of *u* and *me*.

We often don't even realize how much our assumptions influence our thinking and behaviors. For a long time, I was hesitant to say where I went to high school because the assumption made about me based on my alma mater was that I was a rich, spoiled girl who had no concept of the real world. At times, that information would hurt my credibility as a professional and be met with eye rolls and the reaction that "Oh, you're one of them." In truth, I did attend a private high school where many of the families had money. However, there was also a great deal of struggle. The downside of such privilege was that it prevented many from coming forward for help. I remember one evening sitting with one of the more popular boys who was known as the resident student counselor, the "Dear Abby" of his class, and he said to me, "Here's the thing, Kristin. Nobody really wants to hear about other people's shit, and if you go to our school, you aren't allowed to have shit in the first place. So the best thing to do is to just not talk about your shit."

His words resonated with me for years. In a lot of ways, it was true. It wasn't safe to talk about the *not-OK* (my term for trauma and other damaging occurrences) that people were experiencing. I had many friends who were suffering from parents' divorces, parents' extramarital affairs, alcoholism and drug use in the home, abuse and domestic violence in the home, suicidal thoughts as a result of not getting straight *A*s or making the varsity squad, sexual assault, neglect, absent parents— and unfortunately, the list goes on and on. Many who were suffering did not seek help because the assumption was that rich people don't have trauma, so all the students and families at my high school should be just fine. So, these kids were left to their own devices to manage the stress associated with their experiences. How lonely and isolating that was for many of us.

I think this happens in more settings than we care to think about. The suicide rate in my state is off the charts. I am truly concerned about the messages we do and don't send to kids who are struggling, and I worry how much our easy assumptions affect the choices our students are making.

I'm no longer hesitant to say where I went to high school. I am proud to be a graduate of Gonzaga Preparatory School, and I am grateful for the Class of '89 because we are good people who do good things. The takeaway from all this is that assumptions cause problems and affect safety. Remember that trauma does *not* discriminate. It has no bounds. It happens in all communities, all cultures, and all settings. Trauma doesn't care what race we are, what religion we practice, where we live, what our family makeup is, what our sexual orientation or identity is, or what our role in society is.

Trauma is nondiscriminatory. It affects us all equally.

Where we do tend to see discrimination is in our systems' *responses* to trauma—and, increasingly, assumptions play a key role in influencing those responses. We need to be mindful of how our assumptions can become barriers for students who are desperately in need of help.

Assumptions About Our Students

Sadly, I see this play out all the time. We are quick to make judgments based on how someone is dressed, where a person lives, or how a person acts. It is easy to fall into that place of labeling or categorizing to make sense of something or someone, especially if it is outside our comfort zone or unfamiliar to us.

For example, when I am working in a school populated with students of high socioeconomic status (SES) and I encounter a difficult student, the assumption often made is that the student is "spoiled and entitled." If I work with a similarly behaving student in a lower-SES school supported by Title I funding, the assumption is frequently that "this student has had a rough life, so this behavior is to be expected." It's quite possible that neither is true! All we know for sure is that each student is struggling—with academics, with behavior, with attendance, or whatever.

In this case, we have limited information. What if the student is experiencing toxic stress resulting from a background of trauma? It's quite possible, based on the data we've collected on adverse childhood experiences (ACEs) over the years. We don't know the details of this child's plight, and we don't really need to. Instead of making assumptions to fill in the blanks and help us manage our own discomfort (unknowns and "blanks" and mysteries tend to trigger us as adults), we ought to embrace the reality that this student has unmet needs and is asking for help. It's our responsibility to find a way to meet those needs and provide that help. Falling back on assumptions about students based on limited information causes problems. We must be careful about how we think about—and talk about—our students.

A couple of years back, a high school math teacher in a building I was supporting had reached the frustration point with a particularly difficult student. A well-intentioned teacher who wanted to do right by his kids, he was irked that this young man was frequently absent, needed constant redirection, and consumed much of his time. He asked me to observe in the class and provide some feedback. While I was visiting his classroom, I watched this teacher positively engage and teach this student. Meanwhile, with the teacher's attention diverted, two other students in the class thoroughly disrespected another, and a third student blatantly defied the teacher's directions in front of the whole class. Those infractions, interestingly, went unaddressed. The "difficult" student, meanwhile, engaged productively in his task and focused on learning.

When it came time for us to debrief, the teacher exhaled, "Do you see what I'm dealing with? He's exhausting! Is there anything I can do to reach him better?" Confused, I asked the teacher if anything might have occurred in their 1:1 interactions that I had missed. Had the student cussed at him? Thrown his assignment on the floor? Ignored his directions? He replied, "Well, no." I told him, "I saw nothing but awesome. You did a great job of engaging and relating to this student, and he was connected to you, and as a result, he learned. You handled him beautifully."

Then, to the teacher's surprise, I expressed concern about some of the other events that had transpired while he was working his magic with the "difficult" student. His eyes widened in a powerful moment of reflection. He realized that the strong relationships he had with the other students had led him to believe that they were behaving OK and getting work done—in essence, that they were always fine. Because he felt disconnected from this one young man, he always assumed their interactions were stressful, negative, and unproductive.

This teacher's assumptions (or "systems of meaning"—to be discussed in the next chapter) about the "difficult" student prevented him from seeing his strengths, and his assumptions about the other students prevented him from correcting and resetting their behaviors. This was such a powerful moment for this teacher. It gave him permission to see a student he struggled with in a positive light, and it reminded him of his responsibility to ensure safety as well as relationship for *all* his students.

The Way We Talk

Assumptions can truly influence a school's culture and safety. Think about it. How often do you hear things about students, staff, or families that derail a setting or influence the mood of a room? Some recent statements I have heard that are driven by assumptions are

- "If it's a kid from those apartment buildings, you know she's going to be trouble."
- "That student is just seeking attention—he isn't really going to kill himself."
- "That family always has someone in jail; wonder when it will be her turn?"
- "That child is so-and-so's son. You don't want to mess with that parent."

- "We can't suspend that student; her parents are key figures in our community."
- "I'm not going to say anything. The last thing I need is to be on that staff's bad side."
- "The principal never does anything here. If you want to do something, you have to do it yourself."

Consider the effect of these statements against the backdrop of wanting to—*needing* to—create a physically and emotionally safe environment for adults and students. Can you see how these simple statements, borne from misinformation, perhaps spoken in jest or as an expression of stress, and fueled by wild assumptions, affect the safety of the very people we're trying to protect?

What if we were to rephrase the comments above through a responsible, rational safety filter? Might they then enhance the feelings of safety around campus?

- "Let's see if we can help that student rise to our expectations this year."
- "We have to take threats of suicide very seriously; safety is our number one priority."
- "I wonder what her goals are for her life. Have you asked her?"
- "His parent is a strong advocate for their family. She could be a real asset to you."
- "Partnering with her family will help us make headway with this young lady."
- "It's essential that we speak freely and exchange ideas about how to be more successful."
- "Have you shared your needs with the principal? The best thing we can do is work together."

A Spectrum of Trauma-Savvy Practices

Being a trauma-informed school is the current trend. Whereas a few years ago no one in education wanted to touch the term *trauma* with a 10-foot pole, now it's the hot buzzword. Schools, districts, and even entire states are touting themselves as "trauma-informed," "trauma-sensitive," "trauma-ready," or any one of a number of labels. To a certain extent, this makes me super-excited, because I know the effect of childhood trauma and how important it is to create a safe, predictable, and consistent environment for our students and families.

At the same time, this emphasis on "trauma" makes me nervous. Are we diluting the term's power by throwing it around haphazardly? Do we have an agreed-upon definition of these phrases? Have we consented to a blueprint of services, or are we simply making this up as we go along? This work has been my passion for years, so I know that it can be counterproductive to use terms carelessly, to tout programs and strategies that haven't been field-tested or researched, and to overstate our understanding and readiness to truly dig in to this arena. I encourage schools to be mindful of how they describe and define themselves. We need to look at our levels of safety and at the predictability and consistency of our practices to ensure that we really are what we say we are.

Sadly, I have done too many observations and consultations in schools that claim to be trauma-sensitive only to find that they are far from it. Those have been some of my most difficult jobs. When our words and our beliefs are completely contradicted by our actions, we're working against ourselves. When we consent en masse, as a team, school, or district, it's important to adopt some common language to describe our goals and the benchmarks along the way.

Pete and I created the Spectrum of Trauma-Savvy Practices (see Figure 1.2) to clear up any confusion on this matter. The terms we use

FIGURE 1.2

The Spectrum of Trauma-Savvy Practices

Trauma-Ignorant   Trauma-Aware   Trauma-Sensitive

Trauma-Inducing   Trauma-Indifferent   Trauma-Informed   Trauma-Invested

	Trauma-Inducing	Trauma-Indifferent	Trauma-Informed	Trauma-Invested
Definition	A setting that not only lacks safety but also is actively unsafe for students and/or adults	A setting that does not take childhood trauma into consideration in its policies and practices	A setting where stakeholders have acquired some knowledge about childhood trauma and are versed in related strategies	A setting where stakeholders have consented to act on their knowledge, truly working together to enhance safety across the board
Behavioral focus	Students are publicly shamed for misbehaviors, triggered intentionally to prompt removal, and embarrassed for their inability to conform.	Discipline practices address behaviors only, without acknowledging what might be causing disruptions.	Trauma-based strategies are used intermittently across settings, including positive reinforcement and safe social and emotional learning (SEL) approaches.	Expectations are clear and adults partner with students to help them safely navigate ways to experience success.
Academic focus	Grading is punitive, students are not given multiple chances to show their growth, and students are neither engaged nor challenged.	Teachers display a lack of flexibility in reaching individual students, and the academic focus overwhelms the whole child approach.	The whole child tenets (healthy, safe, engaged, supported, and challenged) are taken into consideration fairly consistently.	Staff are flexible and adaptable, ensuring opportunities for *each and every* child to be successful as a learner through whole child approaches.

	Trauma-Inducing	Trauma-Indifferent	Trauma-Informed	Trauma-Invested
Attendance focus	There is no effort to encourage students to come to school. Their absence is not the school's problem.	Student attendance is recorded.	Student attendance is monitored and students are encouraged to attend school.	Adults partner with students and families to welcome and invite them to school. All commit to increasing attendance.
Relationship focus	Staff overtly show disdain or indifference toward students as human beings. Minimal effort is made toward building relationships with students.	The focus is on academics, test scores, and the business of education rather than relationships.	Many staff members value relationships and understand the importance of connecting with students on a personal level.	Adults ensure that every child has a meaningful champion in the setting, emphasizing relationships as a conduit to learning.
Responsibility focus	Student behaviors are viewed through the lens of "will/won't" rather than "can/can't." Staff base determinations about students' potential to learn and succeed on preconceived ideas. Staff take students' choices and behaviors personally, and the way they communicate and interact with students may contribute to students' lack of self-worth.	Student behaviors are often viewed through the lens of "will/won't" rather than "can/can't." Staff jump in to rescue students at the slightest sign of struggle. Staff typically see 70 percent of students as having potential and don't view themselves as a resource or support for the remaining 30 percent. Staff see their roles as solely academic and view the development of responsibility as students' job.	Many students view challenges as opportunities for growth. The growth mindset is prevalent among both staff and students. Staff encourage students to try new things and to own their successes and struggles. Staff believe all students have potential and work to help students achieve their best.	Adults create safe spaces where students can learn, struggle, fail, persevere, and eventually succeed. Staff embolden and encourage students to tackle any task they desire. Staff partner with students and empower them to want to do better. Staff work hard to help improve students' sense of self-worth and belief in themselves.

(Continued)

FIGURE 1.2 (*continued*)

The Spectrum of Trauma-Savvy Practices

	Trauma-Inducing	Trauma-Indifferent	Trauma-Informed	Trauma-Invested
Regulation focus	Staff react to dysregulated students with frustration, anger, and irritation. It's not safe for students to show their true emotions, so they may try to hide them from adults.	Students have no safe outlet for their emotional responses to life's uncertainties. Staff act according to the belief that students should "pull themselves up by their bootstraps."	Staff understand the need for brain breaks and choice yet still may have trouble being available for students while also holding them accountable for their behaviors. Staff recognize that students can't learn if they aren't regulated and work toward creating safe environments conducive to learning.	Students have multiple options for regulating, and staff have taught them appropriate times and ways to access them. Students have been taught to communicate their needs effectively and healthy ways to regulate so they can learn. All stakeholders agree to fostering a safe environment where students can get into—and stay in—their upstairs brains.
Other descriptors	Adults rely on the exit strategy and are not committed to the whole child.	Adults may or may not know important information (name, interests, goals) about individual students.	There is a movement afoot to learn more about childhood trauma and what can be done to help students be successful.	The whole team is committed to incorporating these practices into the workplace for every student.
Words and phrases you might hear	* Failure * Lost cause * Worthless * Waste of time * Not my responsibility * Why bother? * Chaos * Never/always	* Scores first * I have to cover the curriculum * Don't have time * Struggles * That's the counselor's job * This is how we've always done it * Sometimes	* Childhood trauma * Regulation * Relationships * Responsibility * Potential * Strengths * Competing demands * Goals * SEL strategies * Safe enough, healthy enough	* Whole child * Differentiation * Success * Let's work together * I'm here for you * Flexibility * Collaboration * Partnerships * Nest * Safety for all * Connection * Consistency in practice * Predictability
Mindset needed to move forward	First, do no harm.	Gain awareness and learn as much as you can.	Be intentional and implement your knowledge.	Collaborate often and refine your practices.

are meant to denote general ideas and descriptions of our mindsets and our practices, not finite steps in a journey. We use the "4 *Is*" spectrum to begin describing trauma-based practices through a safety lens, and we've inserted a couple of common terms where we believe they fall on this spectrum. If you've heard other phrases, we encourage you to plot them along the spectrum as well so you can understand the bigger picture.

Clearly, our common goal is to become *trauma-invested*. This challenges us to go above and beyond and deeply commit to this practice. Trauma-invested practice isn't another category or checkbox on our list of things to do as education professionals; it is a philosophy, a way of life, and *the thing* that brings everything else together. When we become trauma-invested, we are committing to the belief that all students have potential and are cognizant of how stress can disrupt learning and achievement. We create an environment of safety knowing that trauma is a possibility and aware that this may be the *only* safe space for students to truly learn and thrive. We unite as a team and encourage one another to see the good in others and to offer grace as needed for student success.

As you look at the definitions in Figure 1.2, where do you see yourself? Your team or department? Your school or district? Take a moment to reflect on this. This tool can serve as the start of a powerful discussion for your team, gauging where you may fall on the spectrum as a staff, a building, and a district.

Individually, where might you fall in your role as an educator? Where do you see yourself on the spectrum? The mere fact that you are reading this book says something about your willingness to invite this into your practice. So, thank you for using your precious time to read these words!

Becoming Trauma-Invested Requires Us to Change

Pete often says, "Change is a prerequisite for improvement," and it's true. The reality, for most of us, is that change is hard. Even when we know deep down that it's the right thing to do, changing our mindsets, our beliefs, our thoughts, and our actions is a mighty difficult challenge. As you embark on this journey, I want to share some words of wisdom:

• Remember that comfortable doesn't always mean healthy. Just because we've settled into a way of doing things doesn't mean it's the best way to do it.

• Think of this massive learning project as a marathon, not a sprint. Embrace the reality that it may take a while before you see the shifts you want.

• Be generous with grace. As you and your teammates start to learn, think, and act differently, you may be tempted to give up. You'll make mistakes. You'll be scared. Grace can help you through it.

As you work with your teammates, your faculty, and others to create a trauma-invested learning environment, give yourself permission to have patience. As you build your action plan and roll up your sleeves, be sure that the goals and benchmarks you set are reasonable and don't overwhelm or overtax your people. Remember: each day, you can do right by kids and families. Taking incremental steps toward a larger goal is the key to becoming trauma-invested!

2
Systems of Meaning

I first heard of the concept of "systems of meaning" from Margaret Blaustein and Kristine Kinniburgh (2010), developers of the Attachment, Self-Regulation, and Competency (ARC) treatment framework. I have had the pleasure of meeting and working with them both. They did a fabulous job of introducing all of us to a way of looking at behavior through three explanatory lenses (see Figure 2.1).

The first lens of the framework posits that behavior can stem from lack of safety (fear of something negative or disruptive happening or of being harmed) or an unmet basic need (e.g., being hungry or tired). If we feel threatened or perceive a threat or have an unmet physiological need, we will act in a way that makes us feel safe or fulfills that need as best we can. When we are in this state, we are in the part of our brain designed for survival: the limbic area. The limbic system—or the "downstairs brain," as I also call it (Siegel, 2003)—controls arousal, emotion, and the flight-fight-freeze response. When students' downstairs brains are in charge, their capacity to learn and retain information is disrupted. The prefrontal cortex—the higher-functioning part of the

FIGURE 2.1

The ARC Framework: Understanding What Drives Our Behavior

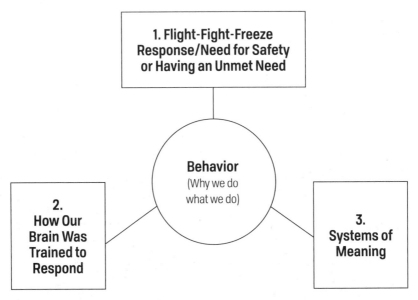

Source: ARC framework concept from *Treating Traumatic Stress in Children and Adolescents: How to Foster Resilience Through Attachment, Self-Regulation, and Competency,* by M. Blaustein and K. Kinniburgh, 2010, New York: The Guilford Press.

brain, which enables us to think, reason, and maintain flexibility—is referred to as the "upstairs brain" (Siegel, 2003). One of its primary purposes is to *regulate* the downstairs brain—to shift into survival mode only when absolutely necessary. When children descend to their "downstairs brain" because of a real or perceived threat, their behavior will follow the flight-fight-freeze pattern. An example could be a high school student checking social media sites, receiving a threatening message, and becoming distracted from learning until that feeling can be addressed. For us as adults, have you ever tried to teach a lesson while "hangry"? Not so good, right? I'm still waiting for the term "tangry" to catch on, for those of us who get grouchy when we're tired.

The second lens of the framework invites us to see behavior as a result of actual brain development. Simply put, our brains are wired to survive, not thrive, and factors such as physical health and secure attachments will determine one's capacity for healthy behavior. Sadly, many children have not had the luxury to develop their brains as fully as they were intended to be developed, owing to trauma, genetics, toxic or negative environmental exposures, or simply the way they were cared for both pre- and postnatally. These factors, too, could explain children's behavior. Children may have difficulty understanding and coping with their feelings, blame themselves for not succeeding, lack trust in others, become overdependent on others, have a diagnosis or chronic health issue that impedes development, or have difficulty reading social cues.

The third lens speaks to the idea of *impacted systems of meaning,* which is when we make interpretations about future events based on our own past experiences, what we have been taught to believe, and how our thoughts have been influenced by others.

Let me share an example of how this can develop. When I was a child, I experienced horrific food poisoning from scrambled eggs. I'd had eggs many times prior with no ill effect, but that one dreadful event tainted my view of eggs. In fact, my systems of meaning were so impacted that I couldn't even stomach the thought of eating an egg until nearly two decades later. The threat that came from that experience was so powerful that even though I cognitively knew I would most likely not get food poisoning from eggs again, I still refused to eat them. In a stressed state (with my "downstairs brain" activated), I was unable to process rationally, and future events were affected.

Our history influences how we respond to current situations, especially when we're in stressed states or unpredictable settings—and not always in healthy and safe ways. These systems of meaning start developing early in childhood and reshape and redefine themselves throughout our adulthood. I have them, you have them, and your students and families have them. They affect who we are and how we interact with others, offering *us* as a contributing factor to our students' behaviors and revealing two eye-opening truths:

1. We construct an explanation for children's behaviors based on our own experiences.

2. Our systems of meaning contribute mightily to the ongoing problems that exist in our education system.

In the following "Pete's Practice," Pete shares a story of how his systems of meaning influenced an interaction he had with a student while he was a school principal.

Pete's Practice

One day, I was called to the office with a report of a fight in the cafeteria. I was notified that the culprits were already in the office, and sadly, I was not surprised to see Dominic awaiting my arrival. This young man had embraced his fists as his primary negotiating tool during the last couple of months, and he'd been suspended several times for his transgressions. Next to him sat a student who had never been referred to the office and was nursing his cheek with an ice pack. As I swept in, I motioned to Dominic rather dramatically to go sit in my office. Knowing his history, I had done the math in my head and figured that he was due for a long-term suspension. "That's it," I told him. "You're done. Call your mom and tell her you'll be home for the next couple of weeks."

He looked at me incredulously, and I sighed. How could he think he hadn't used up all his chances? At that moment, my assistant principal emerged from her office with another student, also toting an ice pack. "Hey, Mr. Hall," she said. "Can you get Dominic's statement about the fight these two boys got into? I'll be calling the other boys' parents."

I stopped cold. Boy, did I owe Dominic a thorough and complete repair (more on repair in Chapter 5)! I'd leapt to the conclusion that he had fought and hurt another kid and that he was going to be sent packing, while he was only in the office as a witness. I vowed then and there to become better attuned to my own systems of meaning, lest they lead me down a dangerous path of assumptions.

How Our Systems of Meaning Affect Us and Others

The experiences we've had influence us on a regular basis. This is how we make sense of the world, right? However, we're not always conscious of this process because it's become so automatic. The development of systems of meaning is a natural reaction to managing stress and unpredictability. We all have them. Places, events, families, culture, media, environments, stories, values, and beliefs are just some of the factors that develop our systems of meaning. Keep in mind, we tend to access our systems of meaning when in a state of stress or in our "downstairs brain"—that is, when we're *dysregulated*. Many equate systems of meaning to implicit bias. Although both imply the same things, however, accessing systems of meaning is a natural biological response to stress: we access those shortcuts in our attempts to self-regulate. Having systems of meaning doesn't make us intentionally hurtful or prejudiced; it makes us human. When we are regulated, we are less likely to rely on those interpretations and more likely to be open to various options.

Sometimes our systems of meaning stem from positive interactions. Other times, they are associated with something traumatic or stressful. Either way, they have an influence.

Negative Systems of Meaning in Practice

Let's investigate what happens when our systems of meaning are constructed because of a negative experience. As you examine the examples below from the five stakeholder perspectives explored throughout this book, keep in mind that these systems could arise from a personal experience, such as something the person has witnessed or heard someone else say. When in a stressed state, or in the downstairs brain, these are the systems of meaning most likely to be accessed; thus, they become impacted and will affect how we respond in the future.

Student:

- "I'm stupid. I'm never going to be good at this."
- "No matter what I try, nothing works."
- "This adult will eventually kick me out, too."
- "I only get attention when I misbehave."
- "Why even try? I'll just be with someone new next week anyway."
- "Nobody likes me here. I'll never make any friends."

Parent/caregiver:

- "This school only calls when something is wrong."
- "Everyone here judges me as a parent."
- "All they want to do is put my kid on meds."

- "This school doesn't understand me or my family."
- "They never listen to me anyway."

Teacher:

- "I've got so-and-so in my class this year. He was always in the office last year. Great."
- "The principal always gives me the behavior problems."
- "Everyone in that family is in special ed. I might as well start filling out the paperwork now."
- "The only thing that will help that student is medication."
- "My evaluation depends on my test scores, and this year's bunch is low. I don't have a chance."
- "No one has ever gotten through to this kid. Why would I be any different?"

Support staff:

- "Nobody ever talks to us about students. They set us up for failure."
- "We are just seen as glorified babysitters."
- "Nobody cares about our opinion."
- "There is no time for relationship. I have too many kids I am responsible for."
- "The kids don't respect us, and no one ever has our back."

Leader:

- "This teacher is so negative. I just wish she would quit."
- "This family is extremely difficult. I'm not even going to try to make a connection."
- "I am the only one who can help this kid."
- "I've got too much to do just to run the building, and now I'm supposed to be an instructional leader?"
- "I can't be everywhere at once. No one else ever steps up."

Do any of these sound familiar? Are there similar comments that you could add to the list? Unfortunately, these are probably just the tip of the iceberg. Remember, these systems of meaning are constructed in our minds and are most likely to present themselves when we need to manage the stress of a situation. If we are feeling overwhelmed, tired, or irked by something, we are more likely to access these impacted systems of meaning.

You might have noticed the language of *ultimates* in many of these examples. Words like *never, always, nobody,* and *everyone* leave no room for the possibility of exceptions, even though in our rational minds we know that—statistically—exceptions are common. In desperate moments, we feel like we're lost in a dark, cavernous pit. Sadly, these mindsets often turn into repetitive dances: the more we face a certain situation, the more likely we are to access these negative systems of meaning, and the more often we arrive at the same unhealthy, unproductive outcome. Have you ever felt as though you were on a hamster wheel with a student? That despite your greatest efforts, nothing seems to be changing—in fact, it might be getting worse? Such scenarios just reinforce our deficit-focused mindsets.

Productive Systems of Meaning in Practice

Now let's look at what happens when we are in our regulated upstairs brain and less likely to defer to our deficit-focused systems of meaning. When free of stress and tumult, we have more energy and give ourselves permission to access healthy, safe thoughts that take into account the bigger picture. We think and act in ways that demonstrate patience, open-mindedness, and partnership with students, parents, and colleagues. As you read the following examples, compare them with the preceding list representing negative systems of meaning. What differences do you note? How might your insights from this comparison affect your professional interactions with others?

Student:

- "I just haven't mastered this *yet*."
- "I have had a hard time with this subject in the past. Today, I am going to try harder to concentrate and figure this out."
- "I think I will ask a friend for suggestions."
- "So-and-so is pretty nice to me. I am going to go and talk to her today."
- "Today I am going to try using a different behavior."
- "I know that if I put my mind to it, I can be more successful."

Parent/caregiver:

- "The school is calling. I wonder what they want to talk about?"
- "This is a new teacher. I will try to be more positive."
- "I will go to the conference and see what they have to say."
- "I'll give them the benefit of the doubt. I'm sure they must want my kid to be successful, too."
- "I am going to ask my child how school was today."
- "Maybe I'll set up a time to meet with the school to let them know how things are going at home."

Teacher:

- "I know others have struggled with this student in the past. My goal is to give this student a clean slate."
- "My administrator obviously sees some strength in my ability to work with tough nuggets. That said, I need to find a time to meet and ask for support."
- "I am a good teacher, and I know I am working hard for my students."

- "All kids are awesome and worthy of an education."
- "Is there something I haven't tried yet that might work? Whom in the building can I ask for support?"
- "The more I can learn, the better equipped I'll be to meet every child's needs."

Support staff:

- "I think I'll leave a note or send an e-mail asking if there is anything I can do to support this student better."
- "Everyone is really busy; maybe I'll just drop by the class-room after my shift and ask a question."
- "I can find three nice things to say to kids at recess today."
- "The more I respect and show genuine care for our kids, the more they'll reciprocate."
- "I can greet each student in the morning with a smile."
- "Working with kids is such an important job. I'm glad I have the opportunity to make a difference every day."

Leader:

- "This teacher is really struggling this year. I need to reach out and see if there is something I can do to support him."
- "Is there a different approach I can take with this family?"
- "I'm the ultimate role model for others. I need to display the attitude and work ethic I expect from everyone else. Game on!"
- "How can I reinforce the value of relationship and the impor-tance of academic press at the same time? We can have both."
- "Next time I'm called to the class to remove this student, I'll offer to take over the class so the teacher and student can have time to reconnect and problem-solve."
- "I've got to assume positive intent in every interaction. We all want what's best for kids."

Now this was a different set of approaches, wasn't it? Who wouldn't want to have these thoughts running through their heads every day? These come from the rational, productive systems of meaning we access when we're regulated and at peace in our upstairs brain, free from stress and worry. So, ask yourself this: How often in education do two nonstressed brains come together?

LOL, right? Hardly ever. And many of our professional interactions include at least one participant accessing negative systems of meaning because of some conflict, argument, frustration, or problem. This is a result of working with human beings and, to a certain extent, is to be expected. Just remember the part of this communication that *you* can control: *your* mindset, comments, and actions. Stay in your upstairs brain, and the positive systems of meaning can continue to run the show.

How Are We Contributing to the Problem?

The next few paragraphs may trigger you, and I am at peace with that. I truly believe we need to be aware of how our biases and belief sets can influence our responses to challenging situations or people. Our systems of meaning also influence whom and what we notice and focus on and how we interpret information.

Here's an illustration of how systems of meaning can affect the way we see things. Much attention has been given to the *school-to-prison-pipeline*, a term that was developed to speak to the high correlation of student suspension with entry into the criminal justice system. Research has found that students of color, students with disabilities, and students who identify as LGBTQ are most at risk for suspensions and expulsions. Nearly one out of five secondary students with disabilities was suspended in 2009–2010, and one out of three students with emotional disturbance was suspended in 2011–2012 (Losen, Ee,

Hodson, & Martinez, 2015). One cannot help but wonder how systems of meaning play into this research. Our country has put together task forces and planning committees dedicated to shifting these statistics. The reality is that many of our education systems are driven by institutional racism and implicit biases that negatively affect our students and their abilities to be successful.

We must analyze how our systems of meaning may be influencing these outcomes. A mountain of research (see, for example, Balfanz, Byrnes, & Fox, 2015; Skiba, 2015) supports the idea that suspending students leads to an increase in the dropout rate, and make no mistake: *we're* the ones suspending kids; they aren't "getting themselves suspended." Skiba (2015) found that school leaders' beliefs and approaches were greater predictors of high rates of suspensions and large racial disparities in suspensions than was students' behavior, and Shollenberger (2015) confirmed that black and Latino males were the most likely to be suspended from school, even prior to any evidence of delinquent behavior.

When there is such a discrepancy between expected distributions and actual distributions, we must seek explanations with an open mind. Could our systems of meaning be affecting this disproportionality?

Could we inadvertently be seeing problems that aren't as significant as we believe? Could we be projecting our expectations onto others and assuming their behaviors confirm our beliefs? Could we be looking for trouble when there really isn't any trouble to be found? Could the fact that we're anticipating conflict mean we end up instigating conflict ourselves?

Minority students, students living in poverty, and students with designations such as special education, second-language learner, or immigrant endure a disproportionate number of discipline occurrences.

Although I believe that most professionals do not *intentionally* discriminate, the fact remains that our marginalized populations face an uphill battle. Discrimination in our systems and in our system responses is real. Because of our experiences, our systems of meaning, and the input we gather from the media, colleagues, or others, we tend to see what we expect to see, what we've been told to see, what we've been taught to see, or what we are choosing to see—consciously or unconsciously. In states of stress, we access our negative systems of meaning, and we need to be aware of it and honest about it. This is on us.

Think about it from this perspective. I have been taught as a woman that (1) I should avoid dark alleys at all costs, and (2) if I enter a dark alley and come across a stranger, then bad things will happen.

So, if I enter a dark alley, no matter why I am there in the first place, then I need to fear whomever I come across, especially if the person is male. Even though this person may be perfectly lovely, I am triggered to believe he is dangerous. I might clutch my purse a little tighter, physically assume a defensive posture, or even say something to display confidence or project a lack of fear. Inadvertently, my actions might actually *provoke* my otherwise mild-mannered alley-mate into saying or doing something out of frustration or dismay that intimidates or frightens me. Indeed, this is a "bad thing"—confirming my worries and promulgating my fear-based systems of meaning, even though the encounter could have progressed without incident if I had just kept walking casually.

Again, when we are regulated, we are more open to positive thought and less likely to access our systems of meaning. It's when we add stress to the equation that we tend to construct and access those *developed* systems of meaning—the ones borne from error and ignorance, survival and upbringing, negative experiences and influences—that short-sheet our opportunities to explore alternative outcomes. In this way, we keep spinning the hamster wheel that leads to deficit outcomes.

Building Self-Awareness

Let's begin to look at what might be influencing our own systems of meaning. My wonderful colleague Joyce Dorado and I have had deep, meaningful discussions about this concept, and we both believe passionately in the need for all of us to become self-aware. We will always carry systems of meaning with us; the key to not letting them take over is our awareness that they exist—if we can name it, then we can tame it.

Read through the list of descriptions in Figure 2.2 and reflect on how comfortable you'd feel if you found yourself working with a student, parent, caregiver, or colleague who matched any of them. What thoughts enter your head immediately? What emotions do you identify? Remember: be honest with yourself.

These are some of many examples that require us to pause and reflect on how we see ourselves interacting in various situations with people who may be different from us. As you read through the list, what did you notice? Were any of the categories triggering to you? In my practice, when I engage clients in this activity, many people become overwhelmed by it. But the more aware we become of the thoughts, judgments, feelings, and beliefs that accompany our interactions with people who have different beliefs, practices, values, and characteristics, the less likely we'll be to allow those triggers to influence our actions in a negative way.

I strongly encourage you to read the first two words in every bullet point below: "a person." Never forget that every interaction we have is with *a person*, an actual human being, a fellow traveler on this journey.

FIGURE 2.2

What Are Your Systems of Meaning Telling You?

Read through the following list and reflect on how comfortable you'd feel working with a student, parent, caregiver, or colleague who matched each characteristic.

What is your comfort level with . . .

- A person who is of a different racial, ethnic, or cultural group?
- A person who struggles with you because you are from a different racial, ethnic, or cultural group?
- A person who believes you are incompetent?
- A person who believes all people from a different race are evil?
- A person who is openly judgmental and critical of others?
- A person who speaks a different language?
- A person who cannot speak or chooses not to speak?
- A person with a limited education or a student who is significantly behind?
- A person with a physical disability?
- A person who is delinquent or a criminal?
- A person who is abusing drugs or alcohol?
- A person who is in recovery from an addiction?
- A person who was raised in a different socioeconomic class than you?
- A person who has a different sexual orientation than you?
- A person who is transgender?
- A person who practices a different religion than you do?
- A person who is mentally ill?
- A person who is suicidal?
- A person who is capable of violence?
- A person who is loud and loves the attention of others?
- A person who is quiet and prefers to be left alone?
- A person who is obese?
- A person who is extremely underweight?
- A person who is wearing a sharp professional suit?
- A person who is wearing pajamas and appears unkempt or smells unpleasant?
- A person with many visible piercings or tattoos?
- A person who believes that education is critical to success?
- A person who does not value education at all?
- A person who is always "right" and never asks for opinions?
- A person who is fearful to make choices and never offers opinions?
- A person who believes that abuse is acceptable in certain situations?
- A person who uses aggression to meet a need?
- A person who believes women are not worthy of respect?
- A person who believes that only women belong in education?
- A person who believes that men are smarter and more capable than women?
- A person who hates animals?
- A person who hates children?

Despite our differences, these people learned and developed their systems of meaning just like we did—just on a different path.

We're all travelers on this journey together. We may be on different paths, and we may have tremendous differences. The one thing that binds us all is our humanity.

I have completed countless observations in classrooms and school settings with gifted, caring, and talented professionals. I'm so impressed and humbled by the educators and professionals I've seen mastering their craft. And I've met thousands more dedicated and amazing teachers, administrators, and counselors at conferences and institutes where I've spoken. Even so, some of the best and brightest still have unwittingly made assumptions and let their biases, discomfort, and fear influence their systems of meaning. Here are two examples that illustrate this point.

Not too long ago, Pete and I were leading a workshop together, and in one of the exercises, we asked participants to write three things that were currently impeding their ability to feel successful in their work on an index card. Then we silently meandered about the room reading one another's cards. I came across one that read, "Too many unmedicated ADHD students in my class this year!" I remember taking a deep breath and thinking, "Wow." Reflecting later, I felt concern and sadness for this educator. Truly, this was someone who was feeling stressed and overwhelmed by the behaviors presenting in the classroom. As a result, she accessed a system of meaning that indicated that all disruptive behavior stems from a mental health diagnosis, and the only way to solve that problem is through medication. I then began to wonder how her mindset might be exacerbating the situation. What role was she playing in this scenario?

Another time, I was observing in an elementary classroom with predominantly white students. Immediately, I noticed that all six students of color in the class were isolated from their classmates, either working independently or daydreaming. When I met with the teacher later for a consultation, I asked her about the seating arrangement. She expressed frustration at having so many difficult students in her classroom, explaining that her colleagues had warned her about *those* students. She told me she had tried to incorporate *them* into groups early in the year but had to separate them because of their disruptiveness. She was worried that the whole class would fall behind as a result. When she had finished venting, I asked if she realized that all the isolated students were children of color. At first, she became defensive, saying that was a coincidence. Because I'd established a positive and safe relationship with her and the staff of that building, I asked her to consider our earlier discussions about systems of meaning. Together, we explored the possibility that her classroom environment had been influenced by the adults' (her colleagues' and her own) beliefs and judgments about these six students and that, as a result, the students' systems of meaning had followed suit. Could it have been that the adults had unconsciously created this new reality? Our discussions led to a powerful team "reset" that changed the school experience for the staff and those six students.

These are just two of dozens of examples I could relate of well-intentioned staff members whose impacted systems of meaning influenced outcomes in a negative way. And my experience tells me that to some degree, we've all got a similar story to share. I know I do—I've been guilty of it and paid for it with barriers in my work. Does this mean we're fundamentally flawed? Bad people? Unworthy of working in education? Of course not! Believe me, this is a tough topic to write about, and I expect it's challenging for you to read about and reflect on—*and* it's vital that we do just that! Consider these examples as opportunities for you to examine your own beliefs, mindsets, biases, and interpretations of your own experiences. This is your chance to become even more self-aware, which is the first step toward understanding how your own systems of meaning may influence the outcome of your interactions with others. Although we cannot avoid having systems of meaning, we can be aware of them and challenge ourselves to stay regulated in stressful situations. The more we can "name" our potential biases and influences, the better we can "tame" them.

The next time you have a rupture with a student, staff member, or caregiver, ask yourself, "What systems of meaning might I have accessed that influenced my decision and this outcome?" Then ask yourself, "What systems of meaning might this student, staff member, or caregiver have accessed that influenced his or her decision and this outcome?" Finally, ask, "How can I take these into account and use them in my attempts to repair?" As we become more self-aware and honest, we can offer both ourselves and others our healthy, safe, *regulated* systems of meaning.

3

Need Versus Behavior

Classroom management. What does that term do to your blood pressure? Your pulse? Did your brow moisten with perspiration when you read it? It's a loaded term, for sure. I'd bet that a lot of us, as educators and professionals, have impacted systems of meaning related to classroom management.

Most of us, if we were lucky, received some sort of preservice or inservice training in how to react to and resolve a disruptive behavior in the moment. We've engaged in professional learning experiences or faculty meetings run by an administrator or the school's discipline team in which we learned the value of providing clear rules, expectations, and consequences for misbehaviors. Many educators work in a school that has a hefty binder full of rules and regulations for student conduct, including step-by-step explanations of the graduated consequences for nonconforming behaviors.

Although those approaches are healthy as survival skills, they don't really get at the heart of the issue. Most teachers haven't learned the in-depth skills necessary to manage their classes effectively, use preventative techniques, and establish a positive learning environment. And most likely, they have neither been exposed to research on childhood trauma nor learned ways to help students shift their behaviors and adopt helpful skills for managing stress. At best, teachers have learned how to deescalate behavior and move on. At worst, they are left to their own devices to figure it all out.

If you were to ask some former teachers why they left the profession, I'd hypothesize that *classroom management* would surface as a popular response. Student behaviors—rather, student *mis*behaviors—are complex, perplexing, and altogether frustrating. Whereas there's a solid research base behind instruction, assessment, classroom setup, lesson planning, content knowledge, and other educational elements, student behaviors tend to be more nuanced, fluid, and unpredictable. It's the part of teaching that most of us struggle to manage. It's the challenge that keeps us awake at night and has us pressing the snooze button in the morning, dreading the thought of yet another day with a disruptive and challenging student.

Can you imagine how much more enjoyable and liberating our work environments would be—classrooms, hallways, playgrounds, cafeterias, bus lines, you name it—if we could more effectively manage our students' behaviors? Or, better yet, if students could manage their own behaviors?

The more we understand behavior—ours and our students'—and what compels us to act one way or another, the better we can begin to achieve that dreamy reality. So let's look at behavior a little more deeply.

Understanding Behavioral Responses

Being caught off-guard triggers an uncomfortable stress response in us that compels us to do something to regain a sense of predictability. In a state of stress, we go into our downstairs brain and are cut off from the rational, healthy thoughts that influence our positive choices. We resort to doing whatever we can, as soon as we can, to try to get back into a regulated state. These behaviors are often not very helpful.

For example, in a stressed state (it's been a busy day, we've got excessive demands on our time, we just had an unscheduled fire drill—you name it), we might *finally* corner Joey and berate him: "Stop disrupting the class, Joey. I've had it with your behavior! You just don't listen, do you? If you get out of your chair one more time, you're going to the office. Now go sit your seat *in* your seat!" How do you predict Joey might react to this scolding?

By contrast, in a nonstressed state (we're thinking rationally, the day is going as planned, we just had a bite of chocolate—whatever works for you), we are more likely to remember that Joey doesn't respond well to strict voices and no options. We might think to say something like, "Wow, Joey, I sure appreciate your energy today. I am worried that all this energy is affecting your ability to learn and focus. Would you like to take a quick break back at your desk to find your upstairs brain, or is there something else you can do to help you get back to learning?" How do you predict Joey might react to this redirect?

Just as we're able to access healthy strategies when we're in our upstairs brain, our students are more likely to remember expectations, behave accordingly, and ask for help in a positive way when they're regulated. And just like us, when students are dysregulated, they are more prone to react in ways that result in our frustration, loss of instructional time, and overall class disruption. That's a pretty compelling argument for creating a positive learning environment, wouldn't you say?

Pete's Practice

I was a principal at three different buildings. In each of them, I heard a common refrain from staff members—heck, I was guilty of it, too, before I learned more about trauma-invested practices. It sounded something like this: "If I only knew what has happened to this student, I could respond better. And if I knew his story, I could connect him with the right resources."

There are two things about this comment we must address.

First, we've talked about the need to create a positive learning environment—a nest—for *all* our students, regardless of their background, trauma history, race, socioeconomic status, language proficiency, or any other demographic or circumstantial factor. So why would it be important to know the gruesome details of their traumatic experiences in order to fulfill that charge? Knowing the details is not necessary. The prevalence of this issue is high; we already know the likelihood that this is affecting our students and our staff. Having those details won't change their realities. We're in the business of unconditional love and unyielding support. Reminding ourselves of the importance of creating safety for our children and ourselves can lead us to create more positive environments and have greater empathy for what our students may be experiencing, giving us a better handle on what is happening in front of us—no matter what has befallen our kids.

Second—and this one gnaws at me—is the dangerously powerful belief that "I'm not the right resource." The reality is, quite bluntly, you *are* the resource. Just because somebody else has letters after his or her name, works in a tiny room down the hall, or took some specialized coursework at the university doesn't mean they've got the magic wand. If you tell yourself you're not the right resource, you've started down a path that leads to stress, heartache, frustration, and rifts. Instead, embrace this reality: if you've got kids in your classroom, you're their number one resource.

Long story short, we don't need to know students' stories. We don't need the heartbreaking details of their traumatic backgrounds. We don't need a mental health degree or access to a therapist to be a safe person for students. Remember, students are having *normal reactions to not-OK things.* Just because they have experienced a trauma does not mean they are mentally ill or in need of a diagnosis. We need to be careful about making assumptions because they can be detrimental to students' systems of meaning and the pathways those lead them to. What we need is to open our hearts and serve as safe, consistent, predictable, positive adults who care relentlessly and deeply about the success of our students.

Beyond *A-B-C:* Behaviors as Expressions of Need

Some of us, especially those of us with backgrounds in special education, learned the *A-B-C* model of behavior intervention: identify the *antecedent* that precipitates a student's reaction, describe and define the problematic *behavior* itself, and clarify the *consequence* that occurs as a result. The theory behind this model is grounded in common sense: if we can figure out what triggers a student to behave a certain way, then we can either alter the environment to remove the trigger or modify the student's reaction to that trigger. And if we can do that, we can "fix" the behavior and improve the resultant consequence.

But I'm going to ask you to go deeper than that as we explore the *why* behind students' behavioral choices. Consider this: Every behavior is an expression of a need. Often in education, we get bogged down in *how* a student is trying to get a need met instead of focusing on what the student's need *is*. We spend a lot of time traveling to Oz—a metaphor introduced in *Fostering Resilient Learners* to refer to the way we get sucked into a student's "tornado" of misbehaviors and chaos. As professionals, we can do better.

I repeat: Every behavior is an expression of a need.

Let's think for a minute about how students try to get their needs met. Different behaviors help them manage their stress, gain predictability, anticipate outcomes, and address various unmet needs in a multitude of ways. When these behavioral responses are demonstrated consistently, we create terms to describe the *student* engaged in them.

Look at the list in Figure 3.1. Do some of the descriptors trigger you more than others? Are you more tolerant of some than others? I'll bet you had names and faces of children for some of, if not all, the behaviors in this list. That's OK; you're building self-awareness! Keep in mind that your past experiences with different students may well be influencing your systems of meaning for dealing with current students.

FIGURE 3.1

Common Student Behavioral Descriptors

- Manipulative
- Clingy
- Bossy
- Dramatic
- Attention-seeking
- Immature

- Aggressive
- Flighty
- Disinterested
- Oppositional
- Prone to negotiating

- Eager to please
- Passive-aggressive
- Overly sweet
- ... Others?

Regardless of the outcomes of the behaviors listed in Figure 3.1, students have gained mileage from acting in these ways. Most likely, the result is that a previously unmet need has been addressed in some manner—probably not in the ideal way. On the bright side, a pattern of behavior can show us the need that prompts it. When we start to look at the behaviors as a means to an end—an attempt to get a need met—then we can begin to respond with more patience and tolerance. Whereas a singular focus on the behaviors can result in negative interactions, thoughts, and outcomes, shifting our lens to answer the question "What need is this child trying to meet?" can lead us to practice empathy.

Four Prevalent Areas of Need

Usually, children's needs fall into one of four areas: emotional, relational, physical, and control.

Emotional need is the need to be regulated and in the upstairs brain. When students are triggered or feel unsafe, or their brains are lacking the ability to return to a regulated state, they attempt to fill that emotional need by acting in a way—sometimes a negative way—to achieve that regulated state.

Relational need is the need to feel connected and to belong. All of us need to feel a connection with others; some just haven't had the luxury of experiencing it in a safe or consistent way. Students will sometimes behave in unhealthy ways to meet their need to feel loved.

Physical need encompasses our basic physiological or biological needs for survival. When our students are hungry, angry, lonely, tired (*HALT*), sick, hot, cold, worried, or anxious, they can be triggered to attempt to get that need met—even if they're not conscious of it.

Control need is the need to have a say. Those who live amid the chaos, unpredictability, and lack of safety associated with trauma often have no power over their situation or outcomes, so they naturally crave some sense of control. This need is often the greatest trigger for adults, as it typically invites a power struggle or defiant interaction. Keep in mind that it isn't always negative. It may include the need to be involved in decision-making processes or to take a strong position on social justice issues.

Now go back to Figure 3.1 and reexamine the list of behavioral descriptors. Can you identify an unmet need that might be at the root of each behavior? As you think about individual students who meet the descriptions, does understanding the four prevalent areas of need help you make sense of their behaviors?

What if we shifted our lens to *what* our students need, rather than *how* they're asking for it? Remember: Stay out of Oz, people! Nothing good happens there. When you find yourself getting lost in the "how" instead of focusing on the "what," come back to this saying: "When in doubt, shut your mouth and take a breath." In other words, give yourself permission to slow down, reflect on what the deeper need is, and look for a positive outcome. Designing interventions solely to address behaviors is akin to putting a bandage on a cut without cleaning it: it masks the surface issue without addressing the core problem. Instead, let's understand the student, identify the unmet need, establish safety, and offer healthy alternatives to getting that need met in the future.

Meet Charlie

Charlie is a fictional (but realistic) 3rd grade student who struggles with the start of his day. His teacher is starting to feel some anxiety and frustration because Charlie's behavior is so unpredictable. Some days, he comes in smiling and ready to work. He is pleasant and kind and a joy to have in class. Other days, he comes in scowling and attempts to pick fights with the other students. He gets aggressive and will often push or shove a classmate. Occasionally, he comes in and immediately bursts into tears and curls up in a ball under the back desk. The teacher acknowledges that she feels as though she is walking on eggshells and that Charlie is determining the direction the class will go every day. She is at a loss as to what to do with him.

What are your first thoughts about Charlie? Take a moment and write them down. What are you curious about? Let's put our detective hats on and see if we can figure out what's going on with this young man. If his entry sets the tone for the whole class—when he arrives smiling, everyone breathes a little easier; when he arrives snarling, everyone is on edge—then we need to help him and his teacher, right?

Need-Sleuthing

What if we put aside Charlie's behavior and started to look at the needs underlying his actions? Let's break his behavior down by need and begin sleuthing for insights.

Emotional need: Is it possible that Charlie's brain struggles with regulation?

Evidence: His behaviors are inconsistent. Some days he does OK, and other days his downstairs brain is driving the bus. He gets frustrated or sad when he isn't regulated, and he acts in ways to let us know how hard it is for him when his upstairs brain is not online. When he is regulated and in his upstairs brain, he feels relief and is excited to start the day strong, smiling, and pleasant.

Relational need: What if Charlie is craving a connection?

Evidence: He wants so badly to be safe and connected to others. Some days he arrives smiling—which makes me wonder if something happened before he got to class that already met that need. Other days, he uses aggression in his attempts to connect to others—which makes me wonder why he chooses that avenue rather than something healthier.

Finally, there are those days when he is so stinking lonely that he just gives up and cries, at a loss for how to feel safe and connected.

Physical need: Is there something interfering with Charlie's basic needs?

Evidence: On days when Charlie has had a good night's sleep and a belly full of upstairs brain–fueling food, he is good to go! He is rested and fueled and prepared for a great day. However, on days when he's exhausted because he didn't get enough sleep, he is stressed about something, or he missed dinner or breakfast or both, he arrives at school physically dysregulated.

Control need: Does Charlie need a little more predictability in his life?

Evidence: Do we know what sort of environment Charlie lives in? It's possible he lacks control in many areas of his life. On successful days, perhaps he's been told what to expect for the day—he has a blueprint in his mind for how things will go, and reality matches it. When something happens that he didn't anticipate, he gets thrown off and goes down a rockier path. His behavior is determined by how much control and predictability he has at the start of his day.

After reading the possible need-based explanations, what are your thoughts? What happened when you started looking at Charlie's behavior through a different lens? Did you feel some empathy for him? Did your willingness to work with him change at all? What if you were Charlie's teacher? How might your approaches shift?

And here's a very important question: Which one of those areas of need best explains Charlie's erratic morning behaviors? Any of them? A combination? All of them? My answer is this: yes. Do we have enough information? Maybe, maybe not. Could we start watching a little more closely to see if patterns emerge?

I think it would be fantastic if our kids arrived at school toting a little sign that read, "Here's what's going on with me today: _____. You can help by _____. Thank you!"

Do you think Charlie has the developmental capacity to tell us which of his needs are not being met? Could he explain to us why he's acting the way he is each morning? Probably not on his own, but we could open up a conversation with him. And when should we attempt to engage him in dialogue? Choose the answer that might get you the biggest bang for your buck:

A.   First thing in the morning when he arrives, so we can direct his day.

B.   When he's dysregulated, so we can uncover the causes of his stress.

C.   When he's regulated, so his upstairs brain is free to process.

D.   Never; he's too young, so we should just observe and connect with his adults at home instead.

If you choose *A*, you run the risk of trying to engage Charlie when things aren't going well and inadvertently exacerbating the problem. And I hope by now you know that choice *B* is a no-go—this is never a time to try to have a rational discussion with someone! Choice *C* is a great idea—perhaps when he is working on something, playing a game, lining up after recess, or having lunch with you. Capitalize on the moments when you're both in your upstairs brains. Finally, I'd suggest choice *D* doesn't give Charlie enough credit. I've used upstairs/downstairs brain language with students as young as 4 or 5, so Charlie could probably share some powerful insights if he were invited to. We need to establish a strong line of communication and connection with our students. Calling the parents or caregivers *in addition to* talking with Charlie is a great idea.

Here's how I'd start with Charlie. In an upstairs-brain moment, I might say,

> Buddy, I am really worried about you and our start to the day. You are such an important part of our team, and I have been noticing that some days, the start of school is easier than it is other days. Do you notice the same thing? If you were to put on your detective hat and examine why some days are easier than others, what ideas do you think you'd come up with?

If Charlie has a thought, then I'd explore it with him and identify an intervention plan based on what he has to say. If he isn't sure, I might say something like, "I'm not sure, either. So, let's be detectives together and see if we can come up with a plan that will help you start school strong. What if we try something like this first?" Then I'd suggest a strategy from the interventions discussed below.

Keep in mind that this conversation is in my language, not yours. What works for me may not work for you, and that is great. We are who we are, and we need to stay true to ourselves. As I noted in *Fostering Resilient Learners*, it's important to identify your "cement shoes"—in other words, your personal ideals, integrity, vision, beliefs, and sense of self that keep you grounded no matter what is thrown at you in any setting. You will find your own way based on your personality and your relationship with your student. Don't be anything other than you in these scenarios, or it won't work.

Suggested Interventions by Need

Based on what I discover in my conversation with Charlie, I might have an inkling about which area of need is unmet. If I'm not sure, this would be a good time to take an educated guess and try out one of the following suggestions. Like a scientist, I'll create a hypothesis based on the research and the information at hand. Then I'll attempt an intervention, collect some data, and refine my thinking as needed.

If Charlie's primary need is an **emotional need**, he will require a regulation opportunity to get his upstairs brain on track. He may need to come in a few minutes early and engage in a breathing exercise with his teacher prior to his classmates' arrival, or he may need to take a few extra laps around the playground to regulate himself before entering class. He may need an immediate brain break to start his day that could take the form of handling something tactile like a stress ball or a weighted pencil or sitting in a special spot in the classroom with some headphones and music to help him reset and regulate.

If the source of the disequilibrium is a **relational need**, Charlie may benefit from a *check-and-connect* in the building prior to entering class. Just like it sounds, this is when the student *checks in* with a trusted adult (a counselor, an administrator, a paraprofessional, another teacher, or anyone else with whom he has a positive relationship) and *connects*. This gives him a chance to talk about his morning, explain what he needs, and communicate the plan for having a wonderful day. This could also be done in the classroom, with the teacher assuring Charlie that once everyone is in class and settled, she is going to spend a few minutes checking in with him. Or he could get assigned a buddy—a positive peer with whom he can do an activity at the start of every day.

If we believe Charlie is presenting a **physical need**, he may need to come in and put his head down for a few minutes and close his eyes. If he is tired and overwhelmed, he may just need a rest. He may also need a healthful snack either in the morning or in the afternoon if lunch doesn't provide enough fuel to keep him focused. Perhaps the classroom could include a special snack bucket that he can access if he didn't have breakfast, or the school could provide free breakfast and ensure that Charlie receives it every morning.

If a **control need** is driving his behaviors, Charlie needs something he can count on when he starts his day. This could be a daily task that he is completely in charge of and that doesn't require another human being—just him performing a task. He may be the official plant waterer, the attendance keeper, the hot lunch tallies person, the helper who picks up the teacher's mail from the office, the entry-task distributor, you name it. Every classroom has dozens of opportunities for little jobs. The key is to give Charlie a task that he can count on, control, predict, and complete on his own.

The interventions we put into place for the Charlies in our lives will vary based on the many factors at play. What is key is that we look beyond his unpredictable arrival behaviors to ask, observe, and gauge what unmet needs might be driving those behaviors. Charlie's teacher will want to set up a plan to monitor his progress, assess how things are going, and address his needs as they change. By shifting our mindset to look past Charlie's *behavior* and focus on his *need*, we can reinforce to Charlie that school is a safe, predictable place and that his teacher is someone who understands him and consistently wants him to be successful. As he learns to trust and believe in this, he will be able to learn alternative ways to ask for his needs to be met.

Adults Have Needs, Too!

Let's go back to Charlie's teacher for a moment. Charlie's unpredictability served as a trigger for her that led her to doubt her teaching skills, her ability to be successful, and her worth to her students. She may be hesitant to try new things, and, as her frustration mounts, she may also become defensive. Now her dysregulated systems of meaning kick in. At this point, accepting help might equate (in her mind) to admitting incompetence. Nothing could be further from the truth! She just needs reassurance from her team, maybe a "cookie" (i.e., a token of kindness such as a compliment or acknowledgment of a job well done), and a place where she can be vulnerable and safely ask for help. That support will help her realize that her reliance on a deficit system of meaning can set her and Charlie up for failure. So, reassuring her that she is a capable and skilled teacher is the first step. Reminding her that Charlie is a great kid who needs her support is the second step.

It is so easy to fall down the rabbit hole of behavior and feel overwhelmed by our tough nuggets. Can you recall a time when you threw up your arms in exasperation, wondering how in the world all these crazy, disruptive, classroom-wrecking behaviors converged upon you all at once? We've all been there—trying really hard to build that culture of safety, establishing a positive learning environment, and then *boom!* Some child destroys everything with yet another tornado.

In these moments, it's important to have a professional support network. Seek out your colleagues in the building, in a neighboring building, or in your online professional learning network to help you maintain your focus. In *Fostering Resilient Learners*, I posed three questions that help me stay focused on those I work with:

- What is my role?
- Who am I working for?
- What is about to drive my behavior? (Souers & Hall, 2016, p. 77)

Adjusting to this lens may be harder for some than others because it presents a new way of thinking and, possibly, a new way of practicing.

Give yourself some grace and permission to reflect. Your own needs matter, too.

We can provide support, encouragement, and a safe venue for sharing our concerns and our professional needs. A culture of safety must exist in all arenas for teaching and learning to flourish. With our network of relentless help, Charlie's teacher will trust that she can be enough for Charlie and that she and he are capable of achieving greatness!

PART
2

Part 2: The New Three *R*s

Back in the "good ol' days," the fundamentals of education were encapsulated by the traditional three *R*s: reading, 'riting, and 'rithmetic. Teachers could focus on those three big topics, making sure to cover the content completely, and know that they were fulfilling their mission. Occasionally, I encounter a teacher who still clings to that perspective, claiming a teacher's job is to share the material, explain the procedures, teach the curriculum, and leave it at that.

"There's no room for all that touchy-feely stuff," a middle school teacher once told me during a break in a workshop. "I don't have the credentials to be a counselor, and my job is to teach—it really is that clear-cut." I couldn't help but think about the late, great Rita Pierson, whose TED Talk, *Every Kid Needs a Champion* (2013), has nearly 8 million YouTube views to date and who said in response to comments like that, "Well, your year will be long and arduous, dear." In her TED Talk, she incisively observed that kids "don't learn from people they don't like." I'd humbly add that kids also can't learn when they don't feel safe. Connecting to kids and helping them feel safe doesn't require extra letters next to our names; it simply requires that we be human. It is in our innate human response to connect to others. Providing a safe place where students feel engaged and supported can do just that.

If the job were as simple as just *teaching*, I'd agree with the old three *R*s. However, we've evolved. Pete sometimes regales me with stories about the history of education in the United States, including compulsory education laws, schools' function as an agency of social control, the comparison of schools to factories, and publications like *The Coleman Report* and *A Nation at Risk*. It's fascinating, and it's led us to this place: We no longer just *teach*. We're in charge of making sure our students *learn*. And the recent emphasis in education has been this: *All* students can and must learn. Each and every one of them.

Which brings us to the new three *R*s:

- **Relationship:** A meaningful connection with another human being—in particular, a student's healthy-enough, safe-enough relationship with a teacher.
- **Responsibility:** A sense of self-worth, efficacy, and competence. A student with these characteristics can engage in the challenging business of learning and mastering content.
- **Regulation:** The ability to take in stimuli and manage emotional and behavioral responses accordingly.

As stated in the Introduction, student success is determined by the degree to which we can infuse these three components into our settings. These new three *R*s enable us to frame intervention options to meet the four areas of need discussed in the previous chapter: emotional, relational, physical, and control. This shift from four needs to three intervention options reminds us that things are not always linear and simple; behavior can be complex and confusing, and there's no single intervention that perfectly aligns with each need. Many students have several unmet needs that can be addressed with one clearly thought-out intervention. Other students may have a single prevailing unmet need that requires a multipronged intervention plan. There's no one-size-fits-all when it comes to intervention.

Here's an example. A while ago, I was consulting in a building and asked to observe a kindergarten student who was struggling with the start of the day. I learned that this 5-year-old was living in a two-bedroom apartment with 15 other people, did not speak English, and had never been to school before. He would enter the classroom at the start of the day already in his downstairs brain and had a difficult time listening and following directions. His teacher was at her wits' end. I knew he was probably tired, overwhelmed by having to learn new rules in a language he didn't understand, and overstimulated because he never had any downtime to be alone. With the help of an interpreter, I taught him about his upstairs and downstairs brain and gave him hand signals he could use to share with his teacher so that she would know what he needed. We then created a morning ritual that allowed him to enter class, grab a timer, go back to a table by himself, set the timer for 5–10 minutes, and put his head down and not be bothered during that time. When the timer went off, he would pop up and say, "In my upstairs brain now" and join his teammates on the carpet. With this ritual, he would usually end up having a great day. This one regulation-focused intervention met three areas of need: emotional, physical, and control.

That is what the new three *Rs* are intended to do. We are all complex individuals with different experiences, and we need to be open and flexible in our thinking and our approaches. Being mindful about the needs of our students will lead us to create truly effective intervention plans. Strategies incorporating one or more of these three *Rs* can help students remain in or return to the *learning mode*—that is, students' mental, physical, emotional, spiritual, and psychological readiness to learn (Souers & Hall, 2016).

Before focusing on the intervention piece of the puzzle, however, it's essential that you partner with your teammates, colleagues, parents, and students to ensure the following:

1. You're taking care of yourself, knowing that your ability to teach, lead, and develop others is compromised when you're not in

peak emotional, physical, and psychological condition (Souers & Hall, 2016).

2. You're embracing a culture of safety, knowing that your primary responsibility when it comes to children is to ensure that they are safe and well cared for.

3. You're considering your own systems of meaning, knowing that your awareness of your own thoughts and beliefs will affect how you process your professional responsibilities.

4. You're shifting your focus from student *behaviors* to student *needs*, knowing that every behavior is at some level an expression of a need.

If this is where you are, welcome and congratulations! I'm so glad you've dedicated yourself to traveling this journey. There is no job—save for parenting—more important, useful, noble, and, yes, underappreciated, than teaching. Please know that Pete and I appreciate you. Now let's step into the delightfully messy world of teaching and learning.

Empathy and Education

In the grand scheme of things, there are two things our students need to be successful members of society: empathy and academics. We all know the value of academic proficiency, thanks to the countless research studies that correlate scholastic attainment with various measures of happiness, job satisfaction, opportunity, income, and social mobility. As the old three *R*s have shown us, we've done a pretty good job prioritizing academics in our schools.

But I worry that the other crucial piece—empathy—is lacking in education. I fear that adults are forgetting to access their empathy when dealing with an unwanted demand or working with a tough nugget. I am hearing all too often a sense of hopelessness about our students' potential, and I see adults far too frequently forget that these students are *children*. Even when students have matured physically, we cannot lose sight of the fact that they are still children with developing brains who rely on us to help them maneuver through the obstacles and stressors of their world.

It's important not to let our fears and frustrations overpower our ability to practice and model empathy. The skill of empathy can allow us and our students to achieve ultimate success. When we can truly relate to what another person is feeling, it gives us a sense of understanding and compassion and opens us up to exploring new opportunities for success. We become less likely to engage in harmful or negative behaviors and begin to experience a sense of connection and partnership. We often treat empathy as a genetic trait, but it is a learnable—and therefore teachable—skill.

I'm excited to see how schools and teachers are incorporating empathy into their academic lessons and classroom structures. For example, I was working alongside a middle school teacher who asked her students to identify a topic that made them *feel* something and compelled them to *do* something about it, and to present their topics and plans to address them in creative ways. Here are the directions for the assignment:

1. Choose a topic or social problem that evokes a feeling in you that compels you to make it better.
2. Identify what causes you to feel this way.
3. Research how the problem may be affecting others.
4. Think about how you might talk about this with someone who doesn't see it as a problem. How can you be open to this person's way of thinking and still feel comfortable sharing yours?
5. Interview someone in the community who is also invested in solving this problem.

6. Name five things you think may help fix this problem.

7. Name two things you plan to do to address this problem.

8. What is one thing our whole class can do to support you in solving this problem?

The students selected such topics as bullying, animal cruelty, pollution, parental divorce, fear of war, gun violence in schools, homework, and lack of kindness in our society. That's quite a list, right?

This powerful project gave students permission to immerse themselves in something bigger than themselves. It also asked them to reflect on their feelings, why they felt that way, and how others may feel differently. The students were so invested in this assignment that the teacher repeated it every quarter, asking students to pick a different topic each time. According to the teacher, the outcome for the class was transformational: discipline issues disappeared, student attendance rose drastically, and overall academic scores improved. The students' sense of community and connection was palpable in the room, and the teacher felt a new sense of energy and purpose.

Why the New Three *R*s?

So, what does empathy have to do with the new three *R*s? I think of empathy as the underlying frame that supports and connects relationship, responsibility, and regulation. Helping students attune to and empathize with others builds stronger *relationships,* which helps them cultivate their own sense of *responsibility.* And when focused internally, empathy aids in the process of *regulation.* When these three *R*s are in place, learning can happen.

Many obstacles can interfere with learning and teaching, such as insufficient funding, lack of materials, shortage of time, poor working conditions, contract squabbles, and—wouldn't you know it?—disruptive student behaviors. Although most of the impediments on this list are largely beyond our control, there is definitely something we can do about that last one.

The new three *Rs* give us permission to pause, reflect, and view a troublesome student behavior issue through a new set of lenses. We're going to shift our focus from the behavior to the underlying unmet need. Rather than try to resolve an immediate crisis, we will look for empowering long-term strategies to support our students' healthy growth and development. With the new three *Rs*, we can reinforce the "nest"—that positive learning environment, that culture of safety— we're so earnestly trying to build and maintain.

The Structure and Contents of Part 2

I want to bring up a metaphor I introduced in *Fostering Resilient Learners*. If we found ourselves trapped in a cabin with a locked door, panic would probably set in, and we would likely fixate on the door as our only way out, kicking and pulling on it in vain while ignoring the alternative forms of escape: the cabin's windows. Likewise, in other situations where we feel trapped or defeated, we tend to pour all our energies into the one obvious strategy that has proven itself ineffective.

Specifically, I'm referring to our overreliance on "the exit strategy"— you know, the one where we send kids out of the classroom. To the hall, to the office, anywhere—just out of here! And how's that working for us? Are we seeing a positive shift in students' behavior and attitude? How about in our own attitude and performance? Are we achieving our educational goals for the precious children we're banishing? Are suspensions and expulsions effectively correcting behaviors and torqueing our students back into the learning mode? Are kids more successful in school when we kick them out?

The reality is, there's no island we can send our toughest nuggets to. We cannot banish them to a faraway planet. Many educators, including seasoned professionals, are intimidated by the prospect of facing challenging students in difficult situations and see no option other than the exit strategy. I get that! Change is hard. But you can do this. *We* can do this. Together, we can equip ourselves and our teammates with the skills to find the windows, learn them, try them out, refine them, and add them to our repertoire of viable approaches.

In Part 2, you'll be introduced to some of these windows—and we'll practice how to stay true to our core selves while helping all our students be as wildly and unequivocally awesome as they can be. Each chapter in Part 2 is dedicated to one of the new three *R*s: Chapter 4 is about relationship, Chapter 5 is about responsibility, and Chapter 6 focuses on regulation. In each of these chapters I outline trauma-invested strategies to target these areas before looking at real scenarios provided by educators throughout the United States.[1] In these scenarios, I explore possibilities for students' unmet needs and then suggest strategies for how to address those needs. The goal of these extended scenarios is to give you ideas for how to address similar situations in your building. Although these scenarios are true and specific, they are far from unique. Pete and I picked them for inclusion here because they represent the kinds of challenges we hear about from so many in the course of our work. I hope these scenarios resonate with you and illuminate your own experiences—and I hope the suggested interventions provide some insight and support to you and your students.

You'll notice as you dig into the scenarios that I often refer to *tiers* of support. As with RTI, MTSS, and other intervention models, the

---

[1]Note that all names have been changed for privacy's sake. In some scenarios, where identifying details of those involved were not provided, I randomly assigned genders to the stakeholders.

three tiers correspond to the levels of intensity, personalization, and specificity with which support is provided.

Tier 1 supports are universal. These are whole-school, whole-class structures and systems that each and every student should be able to rely on and expect. These interventions are intended to benefit all students and result in learning-conducive environments. For example, all teachers might use positive phrasing when sharing their expectations with students (e.g., saying "Please walk" instead of "Don't run") and make sure to greet every student in the classroom with a smile and a warm "Good morning." These supports can also include classroom rituals, whole-school mantras, schedules and routines, and schoolwide expectations that are clear and consistently reinforced.

Tier 2 supports are for students who "bubble up" from Tier 1 and need a little more intentional support to be learning-ready. These interventions may be offered in small-group settings (e.g., a "lunch bunch" that meets once a week to discuss ways to share and take turns), have a limited duration (e.g., a structured recess area to teach particular games and sportsmanship before granting students permission to enter the field), or be informal (e.g., pulling a student aside before an activity to explain some unforeseen changes to the agenda). Tier 2 approaches might also include support teams designed to catch students who are thrust into an at-risk designation owing to circumstances beyond their control. These teams can offer temporary, as-needed supports intended to return students back to their normal Tier 1 spot. Tier 2 approaches help students make positive choices and learn the acceptable skills that will yield success.

Tier 3 supports are provided to students who need more intensive interventions to participate and experience positive outcomes. Personalized and differentiated, such interventions address individual students' unmet needs, teach particular skills, offer useful strategies, and—get ready for this—are often exceptions to the rule. This doesn't mean we don't have high expectations for our students and won't hold them accountable for their behaviors; rather, we'll modify our expectations, *teach* the skills and options necessary, and progress with positive intent from that point forward. Tier 3 interventions might include a daily student check-in with a designated adult, mentoring programs, a classroom job, role-playing, or any other approaches to build self-awareness and an array of skills for tackling life's tough day-to-day challenges. Tier 3 interventions are designed for students who are regularly struggling to fall within traditional learning standards and will truly benefit from additional structures and supports. It's important to clearly communicate the purpose of Tier 3 approaches. We must be cognizant of our own impacted systems of meaning and careful not to succumb to labels and preconceived notions about our students. When done correctly and communicated effectively, these interventions can make a tremendous difference.

You may notice that I don't break every intervention into tiered approaches; this is intentional. I want to avoid implying that there are rigid solutions to every problem, or that my suggestions are the only way to approach a given situation. Instead, I encourage you to cultivate flexibility and adaptability—qualities that are essential to dealing with tough scenarios and meeting all students' needs.

Because collaboration and consistency are important, I offer insights about how to address each scenario from the perspective of

1. The student.
2. The parent/caregiver (anyone who has the primary role of caring for the student).
3. The teacher (including specialists and special education and Learning Assistance Program staff).

4.   Support staff (anyone who plays a crucial supportive role in the building, including assistant principals, the school counselor, school social workers, instructional assistants, the playground supervisor and staff, custodians, cafeteria staff, front office staff, school nurses, bus drivers, and so on).

5.   The leader (the principal, the coach, the superintendent, and so on).

Do you have a goal for your student? Is the student aware of this goal? Are the parents or caregivers aware of the goal? Is it realistic? How do you know? So often, I work with educators and families who are operating from completely different mindsets toward separate goals. We need to come together, agree to a desired outcome, and partner around identifying the best pathways to achieve that outcome. This multifaceted approach should help us build long-term solutions and shift our collective mindsets. Here are some of the mental shifts I expect you'll notice during the process:

- My students ➜ Our students
- Do to/for ➜ Do with
- Admire the problem ➜ Find a solution
- Fixed mindset ➜ Growth mindset
- Awesome individual efforts ➜ Awesome teamwork

As you delve into this work, keep in mind the need for empathy and self-awareness. The situations you face in your current role are going to be different from the scenarios presented here. What works for one student in a given setting might not work for the same student in a different setting, or for a different student in that very same setting. The ultimate variable is *you*. To make this work, take these suggestions, run them through your filter, and make them your own.

Please take the ideas shared here and make them work for you—and, more important, for your students.

Also keep in mind that if you're looking for a chronological list of things to check off before moving on, then you're in the wrong place. Although Pete and I have created a structure to help you tap into bucketloads of strategies and ways to address tough situations in a positive way, we want you to think critically and adapt them to the scenario at hand. Although we all crave the one-size-fits-all intervention, that magic bullet simply does not exist. So, in some cases in this book, I outline a specific intervention, whereas in others I provide alternatives. What *all* the scenarios consistently provide are some insights into building empathy for all involved and ways to collect additional information.

Some educators have told me, "If I could just have you in my ear, I would know what to say in these situations." Although I am grateful that my thoughts and examples resonate and provide a window for looking at things differently, my words are not meant to replace *you*. I encourage you to take or adapt what feels right and walk away from what you know will not work for you. My goal is to inspire your thinking and empower you to design an intervention plan that will work for you and your students and families.

As you embark on this journey, remember to be realistic in the goals and expectations you set for yourself and your students, and keep in mind this quote: "Rome wasn't built in a day, but they were laying bricks every hour" (Clear, n.d.). True change takes time and patience, and we can achieve something every day as long as we keep plugging away at it. So there you are. Now go plug away!

4

Relationship

Three things in human life are important: the first is to be kind; the second is to be kind; and the third is to be kind.

—Henry James

....

Relationship is a human need that all of us possess. The need to connect and feel love is crucial to the body's ability to regulate and feel safe. When we feel connected in a healthy way, we feel safe. When we feel safe, we can learn.

Relationship: **a meaningful connection with another human being—in particular, a student's healthy-enough, safe-enough relationship with a teacher.**

We often underestimate the power of connection and the value it can add to education. Providing connection and safety does not require us to become best friends with our students or minimize academics; it requires us to commit to providing a healthy, supportive environment where students feel cared about and empowered to learn. We sometimes take this for granted, assuming students automatically know we care about them. But building relationship requires that we establish trust, and gaining trust requires that we become predictable and consistent in the way we relate to our students and families and to one another.

We can build relational connections through both verbal exchanges and nonverbal cues. The way we set up a classroom, for example, can invite or discourage relationship. How we greet our students at the start of the day affects relationship. The way we perform our duties within the school setting affects relationship. The way we handle stress, the way we approach challenges, and our overall demeanor affect relationship. We can have such a powerful influence on our setting's culture of safety purely through the way we relate to others.

Many of us entered this field because we are relational people who feel fulfilled when our students respond to us in relational ways. Have you ever had students return years after you taught them to thank you for the support you gave them? Such reminders of our influence fuel us to remain engaged in this work.

Pete's Practice

Have you ever counted to seven? It doesn't take long, so try it now: 1-2-3-4-5-6-7. Done. That was quick. How much do you think you can get done in seven seconds? If your first response is "Not much," I'm going to ask you to reassess the value of seven seconds.

No fewer than a dozen times has the difference between the winner and the runner-up in the Boston Marathon been decided by fewer than seven seconds. And if you've ever stood and greeted students at the bus, at the drop-off line, at the front entrance, in the hallways, or at the classroom door, you know what a powerful allocation of time seven seconds can be.

What can we accomplish in seven seconds? We can greet our students by name, look them in the eyes, smile, and pay them a compliment. We can gauge their mood, capture their attention, acknowledge their presence, and make them feel welcome. We can notice whom they're with, assess their energy level, make them feel loved, and offer a hug, a high-five, a handshake, or a fist-bump. In a vast hallway, running the gauntlet from classroom to classroom, seven seconds can be an eternity to a child. We as adults have the power and the obligation to positively influence those experiences.

And it's the *first* seven seconds that matter most. How we greet our students when we first see them—our facial expressions, words, gestures, tone of voice, contact, level of enthusiasm—those things matter.

One of my favorite challenges I set myself as a school principal was to greet as many kids as possible every morning as they filtered by me in the hallways. I paid attention to haircuts, shoes, eye color, smile frequency, backpack bulk, and any other little detail I could glean about a child so that I could try to say something specific to each individual. I wasn't always successful, but I believed the effort was well worth it. I used those interactions to bring some positivity, safety, love, and grace into every student's day right off the bat.

In one circumstance, this simple approach yielded life-altering results. A staff member came to me after school one day and informed me that one of her students had decided *not* to attempt suicide, despite feeling lonely and hurt and helpless, because of a quick, seemingly mundane interaction she and I had shared in the hallway the previous morning. Evidently, that greeting, that smile, and that connection had prompted her to think that she was worthy, noticed, and real—that she mattered. And of course she mattered! She just needed someone to show her that truth.

Seven seconds. Not much of an investment for such a remarkable return.

I hear all too often from educators that they don't feel qualified to work with students who are struggling or that they don't have time to connect with all students. I know it can be overwhelming, and the scope of students' needs sometimes leads us to feel flummoxed about what to say or do. But there is something powerful about just being human. Students don't necessarily need us to delve deep into a problem or "kumbaya" our way through a bad mood. They need to know that we see them as awesome. They need to know they matter.

Relationship strategy #1: be human.

What's in a Name?

I am continually impressed by Pete's ability to learn names. When he was a principal, he made it a point to learn every student's name and something about him or her at the start of every year—a model every leader should adopt. Knowing someone's name is powerful! I'm not nearly as good as Pete is at remembering names, but I do my best to say a person's name in every encounter I have, whether I'm working with a teacher, talking on the phone with a service provider, or interacting with staff at a restaurant. I'd like to share an anecdote that illustrates how learning someone's name creates an automatic relational connection.

When my daughter Katlynn was 4, we surprised her with a trip to Disneyland. She was obsessed with the Disney princesses, and she felt especially giddy at the prospect of meeting her idol, Aurora from *Sleeping Beauty*. After waiting in line for an hour, she told Aurora her name and how important Aurora was to her. This actress was fabulous with Katlynn, giving her full attention to the exchange. Katlynn was thrilled.

The next day, we returned to the park and again waited in line for an hour, this time to meet Ariel from *The Little Mermaid*. When we got to the front of the line, Ariel looked at my daughter and said, "Oh,

Katlynn, I'm so excited to meet you! My friend Aurora told me all about you and your love for princesses. I'm so glad you came to meet me!" I was stunned, and Katlynn's face was priceless—she was blown away by a princess knowing her name. The experience was surreal and powerful. Katlynn became such a huge fan of Ariel that it took everything in my power at times to get her to wear something other than her Ariel costume.

What Katlynn didn't know then was that the actress playing Ariel was the same woman who had played Aurora the day before. She made a point of making my daughter feel special. Remembering Katlynn's name and incorporating it into an experience was transformational for her. Katlynn even wrote about it in her college essays and considered applying for a job at Disneyland so she could do the same thing for other children.

What's in a name? Use it, and you'll know the power of it.

Preparing for Relationship-Based Interventions

As we set out to establish and tend relationships within our positive learning environments, we need to remember a few key truths. First, although everyone has a need for human connection, not everyone *trusts* relationships. Some students who have trauma histories avoid or fear connections because of the harmful, hurtful, or downright scary outcomes of relationships in their past. You may see this when a student resists your attempt to forge a relationship, or when a compliment backfires. Rejections like these may tempt us to disengage. But such resistance doesn't necessarily mean students are unwilling to have a relationship; it may mean they don't yet feel safe enough to trust it. Authentic relationships take time, and we need to be empathetic and respectful of students' right to doubt us and their need to take it slow. The more mindful we are of this possibility, the more patience we will have in providing opportunities for students to build safe, positive connections with us. Keep in mind that the relationship we're attempting to establish or strengthen is designed to help the student— it's not about us.

How Can We Tell If a Student Has an Unmet Relationship Need?

It's not difficult to recognize when a child is struggling and has an unmet need. More challenging is figuring out exactly which need is not being met. I'm often asked if there are any telltale signs indicating that the unmet need is indeed relational. How does such a student present in class? What might she say? How might he act? If we're to proceed with relationship-based interventions, we must first be pretty sure that we're targeting the right need. In my experience, there are several behavioral expressions that might correlate with a need for relationship and connection. A student with such a need may . . .

• *Require you to be in close proximity.* This is a student who, to get or stay in his upstairs brain, looks to you to provide that regulation. This student may struggle when you are not nearby or need your presence to be able to focus.

• *Seek you out often.* This is a student who often goes to you for advice. She looks to you to determine whether her energy and time toward a task are worth the investment. She connects with you throughout the day, sometimes going out of her way (and away from where she's supposed to be) to do so.

• *Display dramatic mood swings.* This is a student who craves reassurance that whatever is happening is going to be OK, and whom that special 1:1 connection soothes and regulates. This student will adopt any mood to exist in the adult's eyes. He may become a "mood shifter" to get the attention he craves.

- *Thrive from a simple touch.* This is a student who seems to calm down immediately after getting a hug, a handshake, a high-five, a fist-bump, a head-rub, a pat on the back, or any other appropriate physical human connection. If you make a point to safely make contact, especially at difficult transition times, she tends to function quite well.

- *Use personal keywords.* This is a student who will reveal his needs through words that carry interpersonal weight. Both negative ("You never listen," "I hate you") and positive ("That's a nice watch," "I missed you") simple expressions can be an invitation or announcement of the need to connect.

 ## Universal Trauma-Invested Relationship-Enhancing Strategies

The purpose of providing relationship-based interventions is to enhance connection and provide needed support for a student. These approaches are designed to help students achieve brain regulation and, ultimately, allow for learning to occur. The relationship itself fosters better behavior, more consistent effort, higher levels of attention and attendance, and a more positive attitude and eventually leads students to greater success in the classroom. Although there are strategies specific to students who have relational needs, I have compiled some here that are just good practice for all educators to use, all the time, with everyone.

1. Say "Good morning." What better way to start a conversation than to wish someone well, acknowledge their presence, and offer a dash of good cheer? Heck, this could be the *entire* conversation!

2. Smile. Nothing invites a connection more naturally and more honestly than a simple smile. As Pete often asks, "When is 17 greater than 34?" Some claim it takes only 17 facial muscles to smile, as opposed to 34 to frown. So do the easy thing and put a welcoming expression on your face. At the very least, smiles are contagious and make us all feel a little happier, a little brighter.

3. Ask questions. From "How are you today?" to "If you had a magical power, what would it be?" there are a bazillion questions you can ask a young person. Asking questions shows interest in them as individuals, grants them the opportunity to take charge and talk about something if they feel like it, and gives you some terrific insight into who they are. If they don't answer, that's fine. Pose a different question later.

4. Listen. As educators, we often feel pressure to speak—to explain concepts, to share information, to give directions, and to instruct. While we're speaking we cannot learn, so if we're interested in learning about our students and their goals, ambitions, dreams, and fears, we must attune to their words and open our ears and minds to them.

5. Say the person's name. I've already addressed the value of learning names, and you don't have to be a Disney princess to do it! This is especially important when working with children, as it shows genuine caring for who they are as individuals. You can only get away with "young man" and "young lady" for so long.

6. Say something kind. We could all use a little more kindness in our world. How much better do you feel after someone says a kind word or offers an unexpected compliment? What an effect we could have by inserting a simple "Thank you," "Wow, your smile lights up a room," or "I have been waiting all day to see you." Simple kindness reassures a person that he or she belongs in this world and that the world is a better place for his or her presence.

7. Give hugs, high-fives, and handshakes. Fist-bumps, shoulder-taps, and head-rubs work, too. It's incredible how many human beings crave contact with others. Through appropriate, boundary-respecting touch, we can offer reassurance and safety to our students.

I once high-fived a TSA agent at the airport and thanked her for her service. She replied, "You know, you are the first nonemployee to say something to me during my whole shift. Thank you."

8. Whisper-wish. This is one of my all-time favorite relational strategies. Start the day by beckoning a student, a group of students, or the entire class over to you and whispering, "Ooh, I have a wish for you today: I wish that you [or each of you] will _____." The wish could be for students to express kindness to a teammate, learn three new sight words, clean up after themselves, read a story they enjoy, say hi to someone they rarely speak with, or anything else that you'd like to establish as an expectation. At the end of the day, simply ask, "Did my wish for you come true?" This is a handy strategy to use to bridge a long weekend. It provides a positive goal and an opportunity for you to instill a hope and a wish that can come true if the student chooses to let it.

9. Work as a team. This is a goal that I would love everyone to work toward. Not only are we all travelers on this planet together, but we're also a team—as a staff, as educators, as members of this classroom—and our success is up to us to achieve together. As professionals, let's commit to kindness, to grace, to the success of all our students, and to helping one another. This work is too demanding to do alone.

10. Offer tangibles. Sometimes, sharing a physical item with someone else can strengthen a connection. A stuffed animal, a worry stone, or a positive message written on a card can represent you and your care for another person, especially in your absence. Let's look at an example of this.

Chrissy was a 2nd grader who depended heavily on her teacher for regulation. If her teacher was right there, Chrissy did great. But when the teacher separated from Chrissy, Chrissy would become distraught, shut down, and, at times, become so disruptive that she needed to be removed.

Chrissy's teacher knew that her home life was unsafe and unpredictable, and she was thankful that Chrissy felt a connection to her. In my consultation with the teacher, we brainstormed a way for her and Chrissy to maintain connection even when they weren't next to each other. The teacher gave Chrissy a piece of soft felt and said,

> Chrissy, I know how important it is for you to be next to me, and I know how safe it makes you feel. I also know that when you are feeling safe, you are learning, which is your job. I am so proud of the successes you have made this year, and I am so grateful to be your teacher. We have spent enough time together now that I hope you believe that I care for you. I think it's time that we help you start to trust that. I also need to have you learn to share me with the other students. They have allowed us to spend more time together because they know how much you need me. It is time for me to give some of that love to others in the class, too. So, I got you this piece of felt. This represents my hugs to you. Whenever you are missing me or worried I don't care, I want you to rub that felt and know I am with you. Do you think you can do this?

Thankfully, Chrissy agreed to try. Every time the teacher sensed Chrissy's increasing anxiety from being away from her, the teacher would simply rub her fingers together, cuing Chrissy to rub the felt. The teacher would always circle back when she could to provide reassurance to Chrissy. Over time, the teacher was able to increase the duration of their periods of separation.

Ten years later, Chrissy stood on a podium at her high school graduation ceremony as valedictorian of her class. As she started to give her speech, she held up a piece of felt and said,

> I am here today because of this—because someone in my life cared enough to love me through my hardest times and believed enough in me to help me trust and be successful. I have had this felt since 2nd grade and have kept it with me to remind me that I am lovable, that someone wanted to hug me even when she couldn't. This felt has gotten me through some tough times. I have carried it with me everywhere and slept with it under my pillow, and I share it with you today to remind our teachers that their care for us matters. Thank you for caring.

Scenarios for Us to Process Together

During the last several years, I've been able to provide support directly to teachers, teams, and schools through my consulting work. Often, educators present me with scenarios they're facing and request a new perspective, some ideas, or some options for addressing their challenges. In the following pages, I share three such scenarios—one at the elementary school level, one at the middle school level, and one at the high school level—for us to investigate together. We will make observations, analyze root causes, ask follow-up questions, and form hypotheses. To help you process and act on similar scenarios you face in your work, I add my own two cents with a series of possible interventions focused on building and maintaining essential relationships.

Scenario #1 (Elementary School): The Case of Amber

Amber is a 4th grade student whose parents are going through a messy divorce. They often argue on the school grounds and in front of other students and parents. Amber is quiet and withdrawn and not engaged in learning. She isn't completing her assignments and seems to have an excuse for everything. Her parents are responsive to school personnel, but each one blames the other for any concern brought to their attention.

What makes me think Amber requires a relationship-based intervention? The two people Amber needs to be able to count on are distracted by their own displeasure with each other, and Amber is affected by that. Because her world is unpredictable right now, she is looking for something to rely on—namely, a connection with an adult who recognizes her needs and isn't distracted by his or her own. Although her parents love her, Amber needs additional support to navigate through her current situation. If she had a safe, predictable, consistent adult at school who could focus on *her*, then she'd have some support she could count on every day to help offset some of her current stressors.

It's possible that my interpretation of Amber's needs is off-target, but the truth is, there's no formula, no magic wand, no way of knowing in advance exactly what's going to work best with our students. If I'm correct, then using strategies to build and strengthen relationship with Amber will likely yield positive results. If we don't see the results we're looking for after a couple of weeks of consistent, focused attempts, we can try either different relationship-building strategies or strategies addressing one of the other two *R*s: responsibility or regulation.

What additional information can we gather? All right, detectives, let's see if we can create a workable hypothesis regarding Amber's needs. First, I have some questions—and you probably do, too—to clarify the situation. Too often in education, we jump to a solution before we have all the pertinent information. We are so invested in making things better, *fast*, that we sometimes miss key elements that could lead us to the best response. Keep in mind that we may not always get *all* the answers we seek, and we have an obligation to ensure that we're operating with enough knowledge to make informed, intentional, invested decisions. The following are questions I'd seek to answer in this scenario. What questions might you add? Remember: when working with our tough nuggets, information is gold!

• How often do Amber's parents bring their conflicts to the school?

• Is Amber alone in this, or does she have siblings? If she does have siblings, are they older or younger? Are they at the same school?

• How are Amber's parents viewed in the community? Are they influential adults who are well respected, or are they seen as unfit parents who create drama? Or do they fall somewhere in between?

• What was Amber like before all the drama started? Is this new behavior, or has she been like this for quite some time?

Building Empathy and Exploring Amber's Scenario from Five Perspectives

Now let's explore Amber's scenario from the perspective of five stakeholders: the student, the parent/caregiver, the teacher, support staff, and the leader.

Student: Amber is likely struggling with all that is happening in her life outside school. She probably feels torn between both parents and as though she should somehow be able to fix their conflicts. We might wonder if her unwillingness to own her behavior stems from her parents' tendency to blame each other for Amber's choices rather than working with her to address the issue. Their own behavior may be inadvertently reinforcing hers. Does she have a "champion" (more on this later) or someone who can help her manage her stress, or is she all alone in this experience? Her tendency to shut down and avoid learning may stem directly from her feelings of isolation and loneliness. Divorce is hard on children, and if this is a particularly complicated one, it may make it even harder for Amber to adjust to the change.

Parent/caregiver: Amber's parents are really struggling. Both seem to have a strong need for validation, and they feel angry at and hurt by each other. These adults are so determined to make sure their needs are understood that they cannot see how their behaviors may be affecting others, including their daughter. They are even willing to share their frustrations and needs publicly, in hopes of gaining the support they both perceive they are lacking.

Teacher: Watching a student struggle is painful. Having a student who shuts down and is unwilling to take responsibility for her actions is challenging. And watching parents behave in a combative manner can make it hard to want to connect because it generates stress. Could Amber's teacher be anxious about the potential disruption her intervention may cause? Is she stressed because Amber is just one of many students she must manage? I wonder if this teacher has support in this building, or if she is isolated and left to cope with her students' needs alone. Is she new to this profession, or has she been around for a while? How is this scenario influencing her systems of meaning relating to Amber and her family? I worry about the stress this situation is causing her and wonder how she is balancing it all.

Support staff: I wonder about the staff that is present in the parking lot and office when Amber's parents are arguing in those places. Do these staff members have support? Have they been instructed or advised on how to address this matter in a healthy and safe way for all involved? Does the school counselor experience pressure from the team to fix this situation so it doesn't create any more stress? Has anyone talked with staff members about how they are handling this situation? What support might they need? Do the answers to these questions influence how staff members interact with and see Amber? Does her parents' interaction in the parking lot trigger Amber before she even enters the classroom? Is anyone supporting Amber as this goes down? And if so, does this person have leadership's consent to do so?

Leader: The principal (or assistant principal) is also in a tough situation. This leader must be open and available to the student, the staff, and the family. He or she must attempt to be as objective as possible and really work on making the school a safe place for Amber. When the parents infringe on this sense of safety, it complicates things: to what extent should school leaders intervene with domestic issues, even when they occur on school grounds? The way the parents are viewed in the community will influence the leader's attitude and response to the situation. I wonder if this leader works in isolation or has a team for support.

Building a Plan to Support Amber: Possible Classroom Interventions

With each scenario in this book, the intervention options I offer vary. In this section, I offer possible interventions at three tiers: Tier 1 is global, applicable to more than just meeting Amber's needs;

Tier 2 offers Amber more targeted support; and Tier 3 is designed to provide Amber with a strong support plan and a safe person she can access outside the classroom. It isn't necessary to take all three approaches; when working with your own situations, pick any that feel right.

Tier 1: In the classroom, Amber's teacher can start to cultivate relationship and develop students' responsibility and empathy by asking an entry question every morning. These questions provide an opportunity to forge connections and prompt students to identify ways to keep these relationships positive and supportive. Examples of such entry questions include the following:

- Tell me about a positive experience you had with an adult outside school yesterday. What made this interaction positive, and what did you do to help make it a great experience?
- Whom in this classroom do you look to for support when you are having a rough day? What does that person do that is supportive, and how do you show him or her your appreciation? What is one way you can thank this person today?
- If you could spend a whole day with someone of your choice, who would it be? What would you do together?
- When you see someone who is feeling sad, what can you do to help him or her?
- What is something you are worried about? What will help you feel less worried?
- Describe a time when you did something you had to apologize for. What did you do to make it better?

As students are writing their responses, the teacher circulates around the room and checks in briefly with each student. She learns who is helpful in their lives and encourages them to reflect on how they can influence situations and interactions in a positive way.

Tier 2: The teacher is concerned for Amber and wants her to see the classroom as a safe place. She is also aware that Amber feels torn between her parents and is having difficulty trusting adults. So, the teacher identifies or adopts a class mascot—a plant or an animal, live or stuffed (whatever school policy allows and the teacher can tolerate)—that Amber can take care of. The teacher then pulls Amber aside during a time when she notices Amber is in her upstairs brain and says,

> Amber, I am wondering if you would be willing to do me a favor. I know what a caring heart you have, and I also have noticed that things have been harder than normal for you these last few months. I have decided that our class needs a mascot that will help us represent our awesomeness to the rest of the school, and I think you would be ideal as the first caregiver of our mascot. Would you be willing to take care of our mascot and ensure that it is safe and loved these first couple of weeks?

The purpose of this option—which can also be used as a responsibility-driven intervention (see Chapter 5)—is to give Amber something she can connect to within the classroom setting. Although we all crave connection, some of us have learned that we can't always trust it. Creating a nonhuman connection for Amber gives her that relational connection she craves in a form that feels safer to trust. That connection gives Amber something she can count on every day that is hers alone and that may make entering the classroom just a bit easier and more positive for her.

Tier 3: Amber needs to build her support system. She needs to have someone safe at the school, apart from her classroom teacher, to connect to and confide in. The teacher, school counselor, principal, and, ideally, Amber can collaborate to identify another adult in the building with whom Amber can establish a 1:1 partnership. This person will serve as her champion, providing her with a safe, nonevaluative connection free of behavior modification. Although the position has nothing to do with counseling or therapy, over time, this adult can help Amber process her stress and take responsibility for her choices.

Amber and her champion probably need to connect a couple of times every day, at least in the beginning. They've got to establish trust and rapport as their relationship strengthens and they work to identify and clarify their intended outcomes. The champion should be available to Amber whenever she most needs a boost, enabling her to make brief, two- to three-minute visits where she can regain regulation.

To set up this connection, the school counselor might say to Amber,

> Amber, I have been thinking about you a lot lately, and honestly, I am worried about you. You don't really seem like yourself, and I have noticed that your learning has been disrupted. I want you to want to come to school, and I want you to see school as a safe place. I know when I am having a hard time, it helps me to have a safe person to connect to. I was wondering if you might be needing the same thing. You are awesome, and you deserve to have awesome people in your life who care about you. So I thought [name of adult] might be someone who can become your special person. You two can meet periodically throughout the day. You can visit and give her a high-five, you can take a few minutes and share how your day is going, or you can talk to her about what you might need to feel like you

can learn today. What do you think about that? Should we try it and see how it works?

Possible Conversational Interventions

School personnel—all of them, depending on their roles and relationships with those involved in Amber's case—have an obligation to check in with Amber, her parents, support staff, and Amber's teacher. The goal of these check-ins is to validate the difficulty of the situation and determine what support is needed. These conversations can be led by the principal, the assistant principal, the school counselor, the teacher, or a combination of the above, depending on what feels right and fits best with the school culture and climate. The following are examples of such conversational interventions.

For Amber: Connect with Amber when she's in her upstairs brain:

> Amber, I just wanted to connect with you and discuss how I can help you be successful at school. I know things are hard right now, and things between your parents have been difficult. I want you to be able to come to school and feel like you can learn and be successful. School needs to be a safe place for you. What can I do to help you feel like you can be a successful student?

For the parents: Establish a joint meeting at a time that works for everyone involved, including parents, staff, and other supports:

> Thank you for agreeing to meet with me today. I appreciate you both and am glad you are willing to do this. First, I want to thank you for Amber: she is such a joy to have at our school, and you have both done a great job raising a terrific 4th grader. I am sorry that your relationship with

each other is not going to work out, and I am sure you have done all you can to try and make this as easy as possible on Amber. I know you both love Amber and want to be viewed as good parents, and I value that a great deal. What I need is for Amber to come to school and feel supported and safe. I need to be able to access you both so that we can help her succeed together. I have noticed and been informed of times when your frustrations with each other have presented themselves on school grounds. I worry about that, not only for you both but also for Amber and the other students. I know that feelings can get the best of us. I also know that as adults, we are committed to doing what we can for our kids to be healthy and safe. I am going to ask that you avoid bringing those conflicts to the school grounds and that when you do come, your sole focus is on Amber, not the feelings you have about each other. Do you think you can do that?

For the support staff and teacher: Conversations with support staff and Amber's teacher would likely be initiated by the principal or assistant principal, whose goal is to validate that the situation is difficult and to reassure staff members that the leader is available to support them:

I wanted to take a few minutes and meet with you all to talk about how we as a school can best support Amber. I met with her parents and asked if they could make sure their entire focus is on Amber, especially when they're here at school. I'm hoping that will help. What more do you need from me to feel supported? I appreciate everything you do for this school and our students. We will run into difficult situations like these occasionally, and our goal is to work positively as a team to support our students.

Ultimately, these relational strategies should help bring about a positive shift in Amber's behavior. Better yet, the benefits of these strategies will permeate the classroom and even the building. Keep in mind that the personnel involved need to be consistent— even repetitive. The problem won't be solved with a single conversation; these interactions and conversations need to happen regularly throughout the year.

Scenario #2 (Middle School): A Teacher's Request

A teacher said to me, "I work in a middle school that has high truancy and a great deal of student turnover. We get new students every week, and we lose students every week—often with little or no notice that they are moving. How do you establish an environment of safety for a population that is always changing?"

What makes me think the members of this school would benefit from a relationship-based intervention? Sadly, the situation this teacher described is becoming the norm for many schools. Ever-changing classrooms and high mobility rates can really fracture both adults' and students' sense of safety. Not knowing who will be there the next day can be extremely disruptive when we are attempting to establish predictability and consistency. Such a situation urgently calls for relational connection, as many of the staff members and students in this situation don't know whom they can count on. If the school can acknowledge this fact, then the adults can work together to create relational consistencies that all students can depend on.

What additional information can we gather? Let's seek out as much information as possible before launching a plan of action; we want to be strategic in addressing the unmet needs here. As I think about this middle school community—the staff, the administration, the families, the students—I wonder what other factors are at play and how they're affecting the learning environment. The following questions should launch our investigation. What other information would you like to gather about this school community?

• Are the mobility rate and truancy issue new for this school, or have they been part of its culture for years or even decades? Time will influence how deep the wounds are for this school and team.

• Often in situations like this, chaos rules: structure and predictability get lost with the ever-changing population, and we forget to wear our "cement shoes." Does the staff have a clear understanding of its mission and identity?

• What measures has this school already taken to establish a sense of safety for its ever-changing population?

• What are the elementary and high schools like that share this school's attendance boundary? What about other nearby schools? Are they facing the same issues?

• Can the school identify some successful relational strategies or structures already in place? How might these be replicated and taken to scale?

Building Empathy and Exploring the "Middle School Mobility" Scenario from Five Perspectives

Now let's explore this scenario from the perspective of five stakeholders: the student, the parent/caregiver, the teacher, support staff, and the leader.

Student: It must be so hard for the students of this school never to know who will be in class the next day and to wonder how the classroom and school dynamic will be affected. And how scary it must be to risk trusting and connecting to others when the outcome is so often abandonment. Do some students resist attending school, reaching out to others, or engaging in learning because of the school's high mobility rate? Are students conscious of the mobility rate? If so, how does that awareness color their attitude about community? If the people they care about leave, or if they're anticipating leaving themselves, it is hard to build trust and stability.

Parent/caregiver: The stress associated with mobility is intense. We see this stress in parents from marginalized populations who are doing what they can to provide for their families. Moving is often a requirement—because of job availability, family dynamics, transportation needs, or any among a host of other reasons—and affects the entire family, especially as children enter adolescence. Many parents fear forcing their children to start over at a new place, yet when they see no other viable option, they may become defensive or resistant to talking about it with their children or the school. How does this strain the relationships in the home? What dynamic does that sense of helplessness add to the equation?

Teacher: How can teachers possibly create a culture of safety with such a mobile population? How can they catch up their students and provide them with the education they deserve when they arrive in the middle of the year, are frequently absent, or leave before the year is over? And how can teachers maintain stability for those who remain? Having to reset and reestablish structure on a regular basis with students can create unbearable stress for teachers. Often, high staff turnover accompanies high student truancy and mobility. Is this the case with this school? How can teachers build a strong team and put measures in place to support themselves in the face of an utter lack of predictability? How can teachers reassure themselves that they *can* do something for all students every day, and that something is better than nothing?

Support staff: Learning names of students and tracking students is a challenge. That challenge increases exponentially when support staff is dealing with a highly mobile population. How can staff members trust that they are making a difference in students' lives and that their initial interactions can make or break a situation? What supports do staff members need to maintain a positive and caring attitude for students and families and to feel successful in their roles? How can they learn not to take students' actions personally and recognize that all behavior is an expression of a need?

Leader: Managing intense change and unpredictability is hard. Balancing the needs of the staff with the needs of an ever-changing population of students is *very* hard, especially when the leader needs to hire new staff every year because of turnover. Add to this equation the fact that middle school students are by definition at risk—because of their rate of development, hormones, and emotional instability—and it's easy to see how the school leader faces what may feel like an insurmountable challenge. What practices, routines, and rituals can the leader put in place that will persist despite the shifting staff and student body? How can the leader give all members of the school community something they can count on every day? What would that look like, and how might it be used to reinforce the school's culture of safety? Further, how could the leader emphasize the importance of school and the need for students to be there?

Possible Whole-School Interventions

In this section, I suggest interventions that could be implemented schoolwide, designed to hit Tier 1 (all students), Tier 2 (those who need a little extra support), and Tier 3 (students with specific and more intense needs). Consider these options like a menu: select the ones you think will have the greatest effect and try them out.

Tier 1: First and foremost, everyone in the school community must coalesce and identify with its culture. Is the existing culture positive and healthy, welcoming and caring? Or is it pessimistic and toxic, downtrodden and guarded? There are ways to establish common, safe practices and attitudes throughout the campus and community. Here are a few for this school to try:

• *Create a mantra:* Identify a whole-school mantra that can be used and spoken every day and defines the mission of the school and depicts it as a safe place to be.

• *Distribute spirit shirts:* Have T-shirts made that communicate the school theme, its core values, or even the mascot, and hold regular spirit days when everyone is encouraged to wear them to school. This can create a sense of community throughout the building.

• *Give welcome bags:* Give every new student a welcome backpack that includes a copy of the mantra and school mission, a letter welcoming the family to the school, a letter to the new student written by current students describing what it is like to go to the school, a letter from the teachers and staff expressing their excitement to work with the new student, information on the area and important resources, parent and community connection opportunities, and, possibly, a T-shirt or another item printed with the school name and mantra.

• *Give good-luck bags:* Put together a good-luck bag for all departing students that includes a thank-you letter to parents for sharing their child with the school, a wish from the staff for the student to go on to do great things, a letter of appreciation from fellow students to the departing student, and some kind of departing symbol that depicts strength, courage, and faith in the student as an individual.

• *Give staff kudos:* Create a format for staff members to recognize one another and their hard work on a regular basis. A hallway bulletin board is a nice place to house these shout-outs and support the concept of the staff as a team. True staff appreciation isn't something that happens once a year; to take root, it must be ongoing and consistent.

Tier 2: To help bring new students into the fold as quickly and warmly as possible, many schools facilitate immediate interpersonal connections. Here are a few examples:

• *Implement a buddy system:* Pair each new student with another student, either in the same grade or one grade up. The "buddy's" sole job is to build a connection, give the new student a tour of the school, and be available for questions, especially early on. Staff may need to select and train students to be excellent ambassadors of the school.

• *Assign adult buddies:* Adults can also be there with an immediate meet-and-greet for new students and maintain a check-in routine for the first couple of days or weeks after a new student arrives. Not surprisingly, sometimes these connections grow into true mentor-mentee relationships where this adult buddy becomes the student's champion. Even adults who are not official buddies can help. Here's an example of a conversation any adult in the school can have with a new student:

> I am so glad you're here! Our school is going to be a better place because you and your family chose to move here and send you to us. At our school, we believe that every

kid is awesome, and we want to provide you with the best opportunities to grow and learn. We know starting at a new school, especially as a middle schooler, can be hard. Making friends at this age isn't easy, and you probably miss the ones you left behind. What do you love about school? What would make you want to come here every day? What are your interests? What do you do for fun? These are all things we're interested in knowing so we can make school as enjoyable as possible for you.

• *Welcome parents:* Does the school have parents who are relatively stable and involved in the community? Is there an active parent organization? Parents may be able to lend a hand or conduct outreach to welcome new families into the neighborhood and the school. It takes just a little effort to build such a structure.

• *Provide orientations:* For new students who have arrived within the last few days, the school can run an orientation meeting before school, after school, or during lunchtime or a break. Led by administrators, counselors, staff, or fellow students, this can be a great time to forge partnerships, tour the campus, explain the ins and outs of the school, and answer key questions.

Tier 3: For the school's most at-risk and truant students, it's essential to identify, monitor, and connect (or reconnect) to them as soon as possible. Establishing a team, perhaps a mix of staff and parents, to focus on this goal can do wonders. These concerned adults can check in with students daily, calling when necessary, offering to meet with families in their homes or another safe place to build partnerships, sending texts or notes reading "I'm looking forward to seeing you tomorrow at school so we can discuss such-and-such," and generally helping students and their families become a part of the active school community. Giving the team a name, like "Thunder Club" or "Be There, Not Square," also encourages participation. This team can help track students' needs and put supports in place to ensure student success.

Possible Classroom-Specific Interventions

Often, individual teachers feel helpless in a school with high mobility and truancy. How could one teacher possibly affect the attendance and transience rates of a school community? Well, guess what? Often, it's one dedicated, caring, welcoming staff member who indeed makes the difference!

Tier 1: Try one or more of these strategies:

• Stand at the door and welcome every student into class. Have you seen the video of Barry White Jr., a teacher in North Carolina who has a special handshake for each kid (Good Morning America, 2017)? Teachers don't need to go that far, but they should let their hearts extend a warm, welcoming greeting to every single student, every single day, every single class period.

• Lead a daily class ritual that expresses expectations for the class and hopes for students' success. This could be a moment of mindfulness, a pledge, or a reference to a class goal.

• Provide a prompt at the beginning of each class period to connect students to their learning. Engage in some reflection that builds a bridge among their personal lives, the day's state of affairs, and the learning targets for the class period.

• Emphasize to students that because the class is a team, kindness and team play are the only options in that setting. Ask students, "What can you do today to help us—and one another—be amazingly successful?"

Tier 2: When new students arrive, incorporate them immediately into the environment. Here are two easy-to-implement ideas:

- Assign student mentors in the class whose purpose is to partner with new students. They will meet with all new students and explain to them the class's goals, routines, and expectations.
- Write a welcome note for each new student and family, sharing excitement about learning, a little insight into the teacher as a human being, and some tips for them to be successful, including safe ways to ask for help.

Tier 3: The students who are most at risk, have a history of mobility or truancy, or struggle with attendance need a little something extra. Teachers can provide that by intervening early, often, and consistently. Here are some possible strategies:

- Call the student's parents or caregivers and invite them to meet and discuss ways to help their child feel successful. Teachers should make sure families know they're reaching out because they care about their students—not because parents will get in trouble if their kids keep missing school. Here's an example of what such a conversation might sound like:

> Hi, Mr. and Mrs. Johnson. My name is Kristin, and I am Freddy's teacher. First, thank you for taking the time to have this call with me. I am glad we could find a time that would work for you. And thank you for sending Freddy to our school; I am really glad he's here, and I feel lucky to be his teacher. My subject is not an easy one to teach, and it's not an easy one for middle school students to learn. I am concerned because Freddy has missed an awful lot of class, and I worry about how this will affect him. I know that school is hard, and middle

school is *especially* hard. I am calling you for suggestions on what you think might help Freddy want to come to my class. You know your son so much better than I do, and I want to find a way to make this class interesting for him. What does he like to do? What is he interested in? I am wondering if there is a way I can incorporate his interests into this class. What do you think would help?

• Arrange a meeting with the student and explain how important his or her presence is to the class and how the student's special strengths are missing when he or she isn't there. Don't wait until the student is failing to do this—reach out as soon as a red flag appears.

• Enlist the help of the student's classmates in communicating that the student's presence is missed. It's important not to give up: the teacher will be fighting some deeply ingrained systems of meaning, and it will take time for them to shift.

Remember, the overall goal for the school—and the class—is to create a culture of safety that will endure despite turnover and loss, allowing for students to get to the important business of learning. Teachers can infuse relational connections into routines, rituals, and structures that are predictable and consistent across the board, giving themselves, their colleagues, and their students something they can count on every day: a message of hope, love, and welcome that invites everyone to invest in learning.

Scenario #3 (High School): The Case of Sarah

Sarah is a sophomore who is desperate for *any* attention, and lately she's been seeking it out in negative ways. One of her teachers is trying to help. She describes Sarah's parents as "not supportive or responsive" to any outreach or communication. Sarah's behavior keeps escalating, and her academics are suffering. Her teacher has listened to her and validated her actions and feelings as well as she can, and she's responded with goals and a plan—but things are not improving.

What makes me think Sarah requires a relationship-based intervention? Sarah is sending a message that she is not OK. She is so desperate for help that she's resorted to seeking out any kind of response, even a negative one. Sarah is a high-risk student, judging from the preliminary information we have gathered. The fact that Sarah's parents aren't active participants in the discussion is also worrying. Are Sarah's escalating school behaviors a result of not receiving the attention and affection she requires at home? My hunch is that she is feeling lonely and hasn't built the safe connections that allow her to express that in an appropriate way—hence her disruptive behaviors to acquire any attention she can.

What additional information can we gather? Let's dig in and figure out what information we're missing. What are some things you're curious about? Which pieces of the puzzle aren't in place? In high schools, with all the movement and massive rosters of students and multiple layers of activities and possible support, it's easy to assume that "this is just how Sarah is" or "someone else is bound to be working on a plan with her." Don't assume! If we want to successfully and efficiently address her needs, we need to gather some answers to the following questions as soon as possible:

- Is this the only teacher who notices Sarah's behavior, or is she acting this way in all her classes?
- Is Sarah's behavior becoming worse over time?
- How is Sarah viewed by her peers?
- How consistently and for how long has this teacher attempted the interventions?

- Is Sarah aware of how hard the teacher is trying?
- When the teacher describes the parents as unsupportive and unresponsive, what does that mean? What evidence warrants such a strong description?
- Did Sarah take part in the goal setting and planning that were done for her benefit?
- Whom has this teacher asked for help in support of Sarah?
- Does Sarah have anyone in the building whom she trusts? Is this teacher her safe person?

Building Empathy and Exploring Sarah's Scenario from Five Perspectives

Now let's explore Sarah's scenario from the perspective of five stakeholders: the student, the parent/caregiver, the teacher, support staff, and the leader.

Student: No question, Sarah is having a tough time. In fact, she is broadcasting her struggles by escalating her behavior and falling further behind academically. Sarah may lack the skill set to ask for what she needs, so she's making a desperate bid for attention the only way she knows how. High school is a tough time for girls, and feeling misunderstood or alone on that journey can be painful. What might be happening in Sarah's life that is leading her to struggle so much and be so willing to put her academic success at risk? She needs a positive relational connection yet has found only a negative means for getting her relational needs met. Is she seeking connection in that destructive way with adults, her peers, or both? How risky are those attempts?

Parent/caregiver: Ouch. What might be happening with these parents that the teacher sees them as unsupportive and unresponsive? They may not even be aware that they are viewed this way. Is there something going on in their lives that is so overwhelming that it is preventing them from even seeing Sarah's needs? Are they also in trouble? Are there supports they need to be more available for Sarah? Are there other children in the home? If so, how are they being affected by all this? How defeated might the parents feel to be getting only calls of concern? How many years has the school been contacting them with concerns about Sarah? Have they stonewalled school personnel because they can no longer tolerate the negative outreach? Do they believe that there is nothing more they can do—that Sarah is entering adulthood and needs to suffer the consequences of her actions? Or are they attempting to address Sarah's needs in their own way, believing it's their responsibility—and not the school's—to do so? What is the status of their relationship with Sarah?

Teacher: It's great that this teacher is concerned about Sarah and willing to seek advice on how best to help her. But how frustrated and exhausted she must feel, that despite all her efforts to help Sarah, nothing seems to be working. Is the teacher working harder than Sarah? Does Sarah want her support? Is the teacher making attempts to help that don't actually meet Sarah's needs? Is she the safest person for Sarah to express anger to? Is she someone Sarah can trust to handle it? How lonely and isolated this teacher must be feeling; I am worried about her confidence and sense of self. Working hard to help students without seeing progress can be so defeating. Believing that she lacks support from the family makes her mission to ensure Sarah's success even more urgent. This teacher craves a positive connection with Sarah and is attempting to find a way to achieve it.

Support staff and leader: Who else in the building is aware of or concerned about Sarah's issues? Are others having the same struggles with Sarah? Have all Sarah's teachers had the opportunity to connect with one another to discuss their concerns and their successes with Sarah? Is Sarah on the school counselor's radar? How about the principal's? Is she seen only for discipline purposes? What role do others play? What communication structure is in place enabling personnel to relay any concerns, so team members can "circle the wagons" around one another—and Sarah?

Building a Plan to Support Sarah: Possible Interventions

In this section, I again offer possible interventions at three tiers. It isn't necessary to take all three approaches; when working with your own situations, pick any that feel right. There are many ways to create an environment that refuses to allow any student to fall through the cracks.

Tier 1: Here are a few global strategies I've seen work:

• *Implement a mentoring program:* A structured mentoring program ensures that every student has a connection with a peer. At the high school level, this might mean pairing juniors with freshmen and maintaining that partnership for two years, so that seniors are paired with sophomores the second year. The following year, the mentees, now juniors, would in turn become mentors to incoming freshmen.

• *Ensure adults are visible:* During transitions between periods as well as before and after school, position key adults (administrators, counselors, specialists, paraprofessionals, and others) throughout the building. Intersections, main hallways, and other popular gathering places can be strategically visited by adults who are keen to see students—truly see them—and build connections on the fly.

• *Post positive visuals:* What are the school's walls and halls telling students? From displaying student work to posting images with motivational quotations, visuals can send the message to all students that they are valuable and belong in the building, as well as reinforcing core values and positive mindsets.

• *Assign champions:* Who is each student's *champion?* I've mentioned this term before, and I channel my inner Rita Pierson (our former colleague of TED Talk fame) for a definition: "a person who will never give up on them, who understands the power of connection and insists that they become the best they can possibly be" (2013). Does every student in the school have an adult champion? Is there a master list of students and their champions? If a student doesn't have a champion, it's time to assign someone to forge that connection. Every kid deserves a champion.

Tier 2/Tier 3: Sarah clearly has some pressing needs. With timeline interventions, the school may be able to build the relational connection she seems to require before things get out of hand. The goal is to identify proactive ways to connect with Sarah; these are the Tier 2 interventions. It also may behoove the school to have some reactive (Tier 3) plans in place so that staff members know how best to support Sarah when she is struggling.

• *Teacher:* A prudent course of action would be to sit down and talk with Sarah one-on-one, outside classroom time, to build a bridge of understanding. The following is an example of what the teacher might say:

> Thank you for taking the time to meet with me today outside of class. It says a lot about your character. I'm concerned about you, Sarah. It really seems like you are having a hard time, and I notice that class seems to be getting harder and harder for you. I'm not sure if it's something I'm doing, if it's the subject, or if there's something else going on with you. I do

know that I want you to be successful and to learn. If there's something I'm doing that is making things worse, please tell me. I don't want to add to your stress in any way. When you act the way you've been acting in class [give examples of recent behaviors], it concerns me. It not only disrupts your learning and that of others but also disrupts my ability to teach the team effectively. I can't have that in here, and I am worried that something is going on with you that requires support. I want to get you that support. I've tried a few things [describe the plan and goals], but they don't seem to be working. I'm wondering if you can help me come up with something differ-ent that might work better.

• *School counselor:* A school counselor can also meet with Sarah to express concern about her situation and work with her to identify a peer connection she can reach out to. Sarah may have some ideas for this partnership—remember, the student is our top source of information and guidance. If the school has a peer men-toring program or a student leadership team, or if Sarah has a friend who needs a friendly heads-up that Sarah is struggling and could use some help, this is the time to enlist that support.

• *Support staff, leader, and other concerned adults:* A case like Sarah's provides a great opportunity to rally the troops in a team meeting for staff members who have worked with or have some connection with Sarah, regardless of position, title, or role. The initial team meeting is intended to identify Sarah's needs, explore some of those key questions I offered above, and brainstorm some support strategies. Here are some possibilities:

   – Send a positive message home to the family appreciating Sarah and all she does for the school, identifying her strengths and skill set.

- Invite the family, including Sarah, to come in and talk with the staff members working with Sarah (or a staff representative of the team working with her) about how to help her be successful, or offer to meet the family at a place of their choice to just connect and share about Sarah.

- Learn about Sarah. What does she like? What does she do for fun? Drawing from this information, the team can attempt to design opportunities that will engage Sarah in learning. For example, if Sarah is interested in art, the team can ask her to create a school project (e.g., a mural or a template for staff to use) that taps into her talents and invests her in the school.

- Identify others Sarah is connected to outside the home or school. When something happens, whom does she call? Invite that person in to help support Sarah, or, if there is no one, look into the community to explore mentor options for Sarah. If Sarah's parents truly are unresponsive to the school's attempts to connect, then identify someone who can be invested and interested in Sarah's interests and well-being.

- As a team, discuss what's working and what isn't working with Sarah. Some teachers may be more successful than others, and everyone can learn from others' approaches. Even if Sarah has a champion, building additional connections could prove vital.

- After identifying a safe, predictable champion, ensure that Sarah and this person have consistent access to each other. Build a plan for regular check-ins and contact.

The school's goal for Sarah is to empower her to find healthier ways of getting her needs met, including partnering with her to identify and commit to her own goals. Her behaviors, although disruptive and possibly harmful, are valid, and her needs are real—it's the way she's expressing these needs that is causing the problem. Keep in mind, she is a 15- or 16-year-old whose brain is still developing and who needs help learning how to become a healthy adult. This is not a genetic trait we inherit; it is a skill we are taught. The interventions discussed are not time-intensive, but by investing in them, the members of Sarah's school community can change her trajectory and outcomes.

....

Conclusion

Relationship is the foundation on which so much of our success with students rests. It truly is "the thing" that connects us with our students and sends the message that they are safe, they belong in our setting, and they are capable of awesomeness. And *we* are so much more capable of helping students when we model relationship and operate from a "we" rather than a "me" standpoint. I am in countless buildings where I witness individual adults doing great work for their students. How much more effective could we be if we worked united, as a team, asking, "What can *we* do to help?"

Our students need to see us working together. They need to know that we communicate with one another. They need to know we're working diligently to create a safe place for them. Be patient: just because we say we've created a safe, supportive learning environment doesn't mean our students have experienced that sense of safety. It's up to us to prove it, time and again, in every single circumstance, with every single child.

5
Responsibility

You should never view your challenges as a disadvantage. Instead, it's important for you to understand that your experience facing and overcoming adversity is actually one of your biggest advantages.

—*Michelle Obama*

Feeling a sense of value and self-worth is incredibly important to our success. If we feel capable and competent, then we are more likely to achieve and push ourselves to try harder.

***Responsibility:* a sense of self-worth, efficacy, and competence. A student with these characteristics can proceed to the tough business of learning.**

Many children living in chaos and stress learn early on to doubt themselves and even blame themselves for their circumstances. They develop the mantra and belief set that "Something is wrong with me" or "I'm not good enough." This can have a major adverse effect on their choices and behavior.

Instilling responsibility requires patience and understanding. To truly hold people accountable and have them take responsibility for their actions is a huge undertaking. Working with families in trauma, I have learned that children in these situations are constantly driven to cue off their environment to determine whether it's safe or unsafe, healthy or unhealthy—an external focus that has deprived them of the opportunity to pay attention to their internal states and gain insight into how they might be influencing their environment.

Intense focus on external factors supersedes students' ability to internalize how they affect their surroundings. This impedes the development of responsibility.

I'm guessing you've worked with students who will never acknowledge that anything is their fault. Could it be because they lack the ability to self-reflect and glean insights into their own attitudes and behaviors? Are we teaching students this important skill and giving them the opportunity to grow, or are we instead hyper-focused on their actions and behaviors?

Think about it: If I am a child being raised in an environment that is chaotic, unpredictable, and at times scary, I have learned to heighten my senses and be prepared for danger. Thus, I am constantly living in my downstairs brain, waiting for the next not-OK thing to happen, and I am depriving my body of healthy development because my brain is wired to survive, not thrive. Because I am continuously in a heightened state of alert, I become very keen at watching how the outside world affects me. What I'm not so great at is seeing how I might be affecting that outside world. In fact, I may never have had the opportunity to self-reflect or gain insight into how I may be influencing others with my behavior. It's also likely that my caregivers and the generations preceding them have never developed this skill, either. Lacking that insight often leads to abdication of responsibility and a self-protective mentality that "It's never my fault."

Defining Responsibility

Let's take a deeper dive into the meaning of *responsibility*, a complex and nuanced term. Responsibility is an incredibly important part of growing up to be a healthy, happy, productive, and contributing member of society, which is what we want for all our students. Responsibility is more than just doing what you're supposed to do. My definition of the term encompasses the following characteristics:

• *Positive self-concept:* If you were asked to describe yourself in three to five words, what would those words be? If you were to ask your students to do the same thing, what might they say? The adjectives we choose speak to our *self-concept:* our vision and perception of ourselves. Closely related to self-esteem, a positive self-concept includes desirable descriptors that make us feel good about ourselves, who we are, and our place in the world. Kids who experience trauma tend to have negative self-concepts and struggle to see themselves in a positive light. They are led to believe that something is "wrong" with them or that what is happening in their lives is somehow their fault. Supporting a positive sense of self is a crucial step in providing students with the skill set necessary to gain a sense of responsibility.

• *Sense of efficacy (effort optimism):* When facing a challenge, it's helpful to believe that effort is inextricably linked to outcomes. If students exert their energy and dedicate themselves to a task, will they be successful? If they hold the belief that they can do it if they try, they're more likely to attempt it, keep at it, and eventually achieve success. The story of *The Little Engine That Could* comes to mind: We need to instill in students the belief that "I think I can, I think I can" (while we shout in the background, "I knew you could, I knew you could!").

• *Sense of capability and competence:* Have you ever heard a child (or an adult, for that matter) say, "I'm not good at math" or "I'm not a good speller"? Such statements are a devastating testimony of one's own capabilities. If our beliefs feed our perceptions, and our perceptions become our reality, then these harmful statements could well be influencing our mindsets and our eventual performance. Responsible kids and adults feel competent enough to tackle the tasks they've been set, even if the tasks are difficult or unfamiliar.

Responsibility is really a mindset, a belief in self that helps us feel and be in charge of ourselves.

• *Belief in control over one's own success:* Pete likes to refer to this as the "Han Solo" characteristic, thanks to the *Star Wars* character's tendency to say, "It's not my fault!" We know that a multitude of factors influence any given outcome. That said, with responsibility comes the belief that we make our own luck, we're in charge of our own destiny, and we will control the things we *can* control and contribute mightily to the result. Many students have not had the opportunity to gain insight into how their actions might be influencing others—or how others' actions might be influencing *their* choices. Teaching students to learn, reflect, and identify the role they play in a situation is key to helping them see the power they have over their own outcomes.

• *Self-reliance:* Responsible students persevere through struggles rather than needing someone to rescue them every time they hit a speedbump. The student without self-reliance raises his hand while the teacher is helping someone else and waits, doing nothing, for as long as it takes for the teacher to come by. Students with self-reliance know there are other avenues to pursue, other resources to tap into, and other steps of the project to start—all better options than just waiting to be saved.

• *Ability to plan, problem-solve, and organize information:* These executive functions are highly useful in school settings as well as the outside world. How many of us would like to improve these abilities in ourselves? I know I would! Studying for a test two days ahead of time because there's a big basketball game tomorrow is a proactive, responsible strategy. Figuring out how to finish a group project with two members absent is another example. And being able to keep belongings, information, assignments, notes, and materials organized and easily accessible is also an essential skill for learning and succeeding. Help students formulate a "blueprint" in their head for any given goal or assignment—give them permission to slow down and imagine what the final result will look like before leaping into action. This blueprint can help them curb their tendency to act on impulse. Having a vision of what's expected gives them time to pause and reflect on the bigger picture.

• *Ability to delay response to stimuli:* This is a big one. Have you ever noticed which students shriek when someone drops a tray in the cafeteria? How students react when a teacher announces a pop quiz? The ability to absorb information, process it, and thoughtfully respond rather than instinctively react can save us from embarrassment, ridicule, pain, arguments, and interpersonal rifts. As I suggested in *Fostering Resilient Learners:* just breathe. Help students learn to give themselves permission to hit the pause button and, before reacting, reflect on what the best course of action might be. This skill will truly cultivate students' sense of responsibility.

Pete's Practice

During my dozen years in the principal's office, I found that most teachers believed in teaching responsibility to our students. I appreciated that this was a priority. I also found that they tended to default to one of two simple strategies that I refer to as "homework" and "pencils."

Let's start with the homework strategy. You know the one: A teacher assigns homework, and if the student completes and submits it, that student has learned responsibility. If not, the teacher must reinforce the importance of learning this skill through the administration of a consequence, usually punitive. As a principal, I often had students referred to the office for not completing their homework. Naturally, I asked them what could possibly have been more important for them to do than their homework. Here's a sampling of the responses I got: students were caring for younger siblings, hiding from drunk or doped-up family members, walking miles to the grocery store to pick up food for the family, taking on chores or other responsibilities, and participating in sporting events, concerts, clubs, activities, and all sorts of other pursuits. I think there's a perception that kids who don't complete and submit their homework spend the whole afternoon and evening playing video games or Snapchatting with their friends. More often than not, there's a legitimate explanation.

Now for the pencils strategy. We probably all agree that students should bring a pencil to class. But I found it strange to have students referred to the office for failing to do so. If only we could show empathy for what our students are going through at home, in the neighborhood, and in their own heads, we'd provide that safe, predictable, consistent environment that welcomes students to class, pencil or no pencil. We'd love them for being there and work with them to help them learn. Having a pencil does not make one learning-ready, just as lacking a pencil doesn't make one learning-averse.

You may have noticed that neither of those two strategies has a place on the list of characteristics Kristin uses to define *responsibility*—which means many educators aren't working from the same page. Imagine the confusion for students, staff, leaders, and parents! As my colleague and friend Becky DuFour says, "Clarity precedes competence." So, if we want our kids to be competent, responsible young people, we—all of us, especially the adults—need to ensure that we clarify our definitions, our expectations, and our approaches for teaching this crucial *R*.

We Can Teach Responsibility

As Pete illustrated, clarifying and teaching responsibility is essential. This process involves not only showing kids what they need to do but also helping them understand why they need to do it. When students can assign meaning and value to responsibility, they are more likely to consent to work toward gaining it. Students and adults alike are more inclined to engage and take ownership when they see a task as something worth doing. Because everything we do should be purposeful, we can shed light on why we're asking students to do something.

Teaching responsibility also involves giving our students a positive sense of self. Seeing themselves as competent is key. When I see myself as capable of doing something, I am more likely to do it and take ownership of that choice and action. I love schools' efforts in recent years to build a growth mindset and foster mindfulness, which tend to lead directly to fostering a sense of responsibility. Two other ways we can cultivate responsibility are to teach students about cause and effect and to choose our words carefully.

Understanding Cause and Effect

Understanding the concept of cause and effect is an important part of gaining personal responsibility. When you are working with students who have contributed to a disruption or problem in some way, instilling an awareness of their role in that situation is key. The old expression "It takes two to tango" comes to mind here. When a student claims something happened *to* her, it's important to help that student identify what she may have said or done to affect the outcome. Here's an example:

> The recess bell rings. Student A runs into Student B while lining up to go in from recess. Student B then turns around and shoves Student A, knocking him to the ground. Student A begins to cry, and Student B is sent to the office.

A huge opportunity has presented itself here. Both students should have been held accountable for their part in this incident. In the repair piece, the adult's goal would be to walk them both through the situation, as Student A believes he is the victim and Student B has become the target of the discipline. We would want to break down the following facts:

• When the bell rang (which itself can be triggering for many students and adults), Student A dashed to the line with minimal body control, resulting in his slamming into Student B.

• Student B was caught off guard and moved to her downstairs (survival) brain and protected herself by shoving Student A impulsively.

• Student A was also caught off guard, so much that the shove literally knocked him off his feet. He may have cried more from shock than from pain. And then . . .

• The crying caught the attention of the adult, who saw the end result (Student A crying and Student B standing over him) rather than the whole picture.

In processing this situation, the responsible adult might want to lead a repair that includes teaching a little responsibility, encouraging both students to take ownership of their actions and identifying the effects of their choices. I don't believe either intentionally meant to do harm; both were just operating from dysregulated states and lacked awareness. Both students need to put practices into place: Student A could learn better body control and spatial awareness, and Student B could incorporate a (metaphorical) pause button. As we hold both students accountable for their actions—because the actions resulted in harm to each other—their interventions could include practicing healthier or more regulated ways to respond when the bell rings at recess and possibly other times when they might be triggered.

Words Matter

Responsibility allows us to connect at a deeper level with ourselves and our students, and the words we use are crucial in this endeavor. I'm a big fan of using the word *and* instead of *but,* which I see as a powerful communication changer that can help us in all our relationships. The word *and* invites connection and partnership; the word *but* discounts the intention and focuses on what could have been better. For example, contrast "I get that you were trying to help, *but* that isn't what I need right now" with "I get that you were trying to help, *and* that isn't what I need right now." The former sends a message that the attempt to help failed or was not appreciated, whereas the latter acknowledges the good intention and extends an invitation to keep trying. This simple shift can make a huge difference in building connections with others, including kids: "I see that you are frustrated, *and* throwing a book isn't going to help the situation." "I understand that you want a break right now, *and* you need to finish one more problem before we can do that."

Another is the word *yet*. Simple phrases like "You haven't learned that yet" or "I haven't figured this out yet" convey vulnerability, willingness to learn, and expression of a growth-oriented mindset. *Yet* invites hope, encourages grit, shows the possibility that things can be OK, and orients us toward partnership.

Let me illustrate the power of *yet* with a personal example. This last year, we have been working on building my son's regulation and positive sense of self. He was on board and pushed himself to try new things, but tended to quit or not even try if a task seemed too challenging. One day, we were out at a friend's property and there was this hose that needed to be wound up—a long, unwieldy, extremely hard-to-coil hose. Honestly, this thing was a pain in the keister. I asked my son to coil the hose as his chore for that morning, saying, "It's going to be tough, and I believe you can accomplish it. Just stick with it." Well, he set out to do it, and it was hard. He kicked, he walked away, he yelled at it, he even cried at one point.

It was such a frustrating task, and the mama bear in me wanted to go out there and rescue him and help—and I didn't. I just kept saying, "You'll figure it out, buddy—you just haven't done it *yet*. Keep trying." Two hours later, that sucker was coiled and looking good. The smile on my son's face after accomplishing such a complex task was priceless—he beamed the rest of the day. He was so proud of himself and learned so much from not giving up. The next weekend, he jumped off a 30-foot cliff into the water without a life jacket when just two years ago he refused to put his head under the water at all. Talk about huge strides. I truly think that his tenacity to coil that hose helped build his confidence to try something new and more challenging.

Sometimes we need to challenge our students and not be afraid of their responses to those challenges. Some of our greatest life lessons come from our toughest battles, and we may need to let our students struggle a little. The key is inviting them into the process and having them see it as worthwhile. Had I just told my son to coil the hose and not explained the chore's purpose and the goal for him, I don't think the outcome would have been the same. But he knew the purpose of the chore was to help him and build on his sense of competence, not to punish or disempower him.

Think of the power in that task. Consider the outcome of it. What appears to be a single, relatively simple chore was really a way to build a sense of responsibility *and* connection. Remember: Even though we all crave relationship, not everyone can trust it. The humans in some kids' worlds may have hurt them, left them, or given up on them. So instead of relationship, we can use the idea of responsibility to create a sense of connection and predictability. We can build connection through a job, a task, an inanimate object. In the classroom, this can take the form of a role like official page turner, scout for the moment, paper passer, or line leader. These tasks can divert students from dysregulating because of transitions, triggers, or impacted systems of meaning that tell them things won't go well. We can use jobs and tasks as proactive measures to support student success rather than waiting for students to fail.

How Can We Tell If a Student Has an Unmet Responsibility Need?

Students express their various needs in all sorts of ways. It's up to us to interpret those expressions—to examine our students' behaviors, actions, comments, and characteristics—and identify the need cloaked within. It's not always easy, but in my experience, there are several behavioral expressions that might correlate with a need to build responsibility. A student with such a need may . . .

- *Crave control.* This is the characteristic I see most often. Students who believe external influences are in charge, who feel their lives are out of control, who attempt to regain a sense of control and predictability—often in inappropriate or norm-violating ways—express this need quite clearly. This need for control is often the best indicator that a responsibility-building intervention is warranted.

- *Seek predictability.* Many students, especially those who have been exposed to chronic stress and adversity, have learned to cue off their environment. They seek safety in the predictability of a schedule, expected transitions, routines, and consistency. If you notice a student struggling when the schedule is disrupted, tasks are altered in some way, or something unexpected pops up, know that this is natural and genuine, and building responsibility can help.

- *Have fractured interpersonal relationships.* Interestingly, students who have been let down by the humans in their world are prime candidates for a responsibility-based intervention. This is a safe way to begin establishing trust and relationship that doesn't require them to rely on another person. We can set up interventions around responsibility, like the hose-coiling task for my son, that give them that sense of predictability without the risk of being hurt by others.

- *Engage in negative self-talk.* Have you ever heard a student say, "I'm no good at that," "I'm so stupid," or "I'll never make that team"? These are indications that the young person lacks the self-esteem, the sense of efficacy, and the belief systems that lead to success. You can build those up through responsibility-based efforts.

- *Use the exit strategy.* Many of our students choose to avoid tasks that they cannot master easily. Or, when the going gets tough, they pull the plug and escape—either by quitting or by behaving in such a way that their teachers remove them. Because of past negative experiences, the perception that they'll fail, or the discomfort of hard work, they're not inclined to continue through the struggles. They haven't yet built a connection among the value of the goal, the merit of perseverance, and the benefits of grinding through tough times.

 ## Universal Trauma-Invested Responsibility-Developing Strategies

We support students' development of responsibility so that they can experience success when everything is going as planned *and* when life throws a curveball at them. When an unforeseen event occurs, how will kids handle it? With the elements of responsibility ingrained in their systems, they'll be much better equipped to manage that turmoil, organize the bits of information coming their way, and create a plan to experience success. There are many ways to teach responsibility. The following are some of my favorites that work for just about anybody.

1. Say *yet*. There probably isn't one word that serves a more universal, powerful purpose in an educator's vocabulary than this one. Using *yet*, as I explained previously, expresses a growth mindset, belief in a student's ability, and trust in a positive eventual outcome. It is a word of empowerment, of patience, of grace, and of confidence. *Yet* belongs in the Word Hall of Fame, if you ask me!

2. **Provide clear expectations and rubrics.** Nothing better helps students achieve success in academics, behavior, attendance, or any other education-related area than being clear on exactly what is expected and what success looks like. Ever shot an arrow without having a target? That's how students feel when they don't have clear goals or expectations to work toward.

3. Set goals, create action plans, and monitor progress often. Knowing where we are now, where we're going, and how we're going to get there takes the mystery out of learning and schooling. By following through and checking in often, we can ensure our students know where they stand in their journey every step of the way. Whether it's charting incremental growth in words read correctly per minute or tracking the steps of completing a physics lab, when the plan is explicit, our students are more likely to follow through. Eventually, to solidify their sense of responsibility, we'll teach them how to take those steps on their own.

4. Let students choose where to work. Not everybody does well in rows. Not everybody does well at tables set up for four, either. Or in chairs at all, for that matter. In helping our students to develop responsibility, we can offer them options for where they get to work. Having options in our classrooms is essential—chairs, desks, nooks, exercise balls, bean bags, sofas . . . anywhere a student can be successful is just fine. The key is to help students identify where they can work successfully, what success looks like, and how to get back on track if they become distracted.

5. Assign seating. Along the same lines as the previous strategy, sometimes students cannot find their happy place on their own and need us to provide it for them. We can assign seats, partners, turns in a rotation, or any other element if it helps our students experience success in learning. Pete's wife Mindy, who teaches kindergarten, is a master of this. She begins with assigned seating (spots on the carpet and seats at tables around the room), allows students to explore different options throughout the year and choose where they work best, and uses assigned seating as a remedy for students who struggle to make that decision on their own. "Are you being successful here?" she asks.

"If not, can you find another spot where you can be successful, or do you need me to help you find that spot?"

6. Teach grit. I've seen a lot of different things happen in classrooms in the name of teaching grit, and I'd like to make a suggestion: let's start teaching grit with something *non*academic. When we struggle or fail, what makes us want to keep going? If we're passionate about the goal or the process, we'll persevere, right? For a smaller child, that might mean tying her shoes, riding his bike, or shooting a basket. For a bigger kid, it could mean playing a song on the piano, learning a dance move, or mastering a video game. Once students have reached their goal, let's help them see that they've used grit in that setting—they've persevered, they've grinded and battled—to achieve success. Then, we can transfer that skill back into academics, drawing the parallel that what got them through level 17 in the zombie game is the same quality—*grit*—that will help them conquer the alphabet, algebraic equations, and a well-defended thesis. Very rarely will teaching grit go well if we begin with tough academic tasks.

7. Assign jobs. Having a responsibility in the classroom—from turning the lights on or off to handing out papers, monitoring participation in a discussion, putting up chairs, or sharpening pencils—helps a student feel connected, empowered, and valuable. When we establish jobs and build a community in which we all understand that we each have a role in helping the classroom run smoothly, good things result. Roles can be assigned according to students' strengths, preferences, or needs, or randomly through the selection of task cards or another method.

8. Forecast changes. Many of our students, particularly those with trauma histories, have difficulty with transitions. Even more troublesome are changes to the routine, unexpected interruptions, or extra transitions. If we can prepare our students for variances in the schedule, location, or agenda—because of special projects, assemblies, shortened schedules, or any other reason—we can help them to embrace the change as a new reality.

9. **Attend to cause and effect.** This is one of those "natural consequence" conversations, and there doesn't have to be a negative consequence to prompt it. As teachers, let's be explicit with our students about cause and effect: when *this* happened, *that* was the result. Ask them to draw a connection between events, especially if the outcome is related to what they said or did. As students build this skill, we can ask them to predict what would happen if we said or did such-and-such. Attuning to this skill enables students to take ownership of their actions and the resultant outcomes, equipping them to make continually better decisions.

10. **Use positive self-talk.** Many of our students tell themselves what's wrong with them and what they can't do, and we need to change the narrative. We can share, explicitly, our belief that students are capable, competent, and likely to experience success. When they know exactly what will help them succeed, they'll be more likely to internalize those positive thoughts and begin to repeat them, also— especially if we focus on fluid characteristics like effort, attitude, and grit rather than static descriptors like intelligence, talent, and "smarts."

Scenarios for Us to Process Together

In the following pages, I share three real scenarios—one at the elementary school level, one at the middle school level, and one at the high school level—for us to investigate together. We will make observations, analyze root causes, ask follow-up questions, and form hypotheses. To help you process and act on similar scenarios you face in your work,

I add my own two cents with a series of possible interventions focused on building and reinforcing responsibility.

Scenario #1 (Elementary School): The Case of Terrance

A school counselor describes a difficult situation:

> Terrance is a 1st grade student who disclosed to me that he witnessed domestic violence in his home between his parents. Because I'm the school counselor and therefore a mandated reporter, I had to call Child Protective Services. Since the CPS call, the parents have been very upset with me and have told Terrance that I am a horrible person who is trying to ruin their family. I work with Terrance on a weekly basis to address his negative behaviors in the school, but we (the school) are struggling because of lack of parent support. It's created an "us versus them" mentality. How do we help this child and break down the barriers with this family? How do we build support?

This is such a tough case. So much is at risk with this scenario: a child who took the chance of revealing that he was unsafe and a school counselor who fulfilled her legal obligation to report the situation, only to be met with anger and frustration and parents who are now vulnerable and fearful. The initial outcome of this scenario is less than desirable, and all involved must work intentionally toward healing.

What makes me think Terrance requires a responsibility-based intervention? Poor Terrance took the risk of trusting a safe adult and was met with the worst possible result: the two people he most needs to be able to count on are distracted by their own displeasure with each other and, possibly, with the school as a result of the call to CPS, and Terrance is paying the price. Because his world is so unpredictable right now, he is looking for something to depend on. However, to set Terrance up to rely on a human is risky, as his disclosure of his domestic situation has caused potential additional risk not only to his safety but also to his ability to trust adults in the future. Because of the counselor's call to CPS, Terrance's parents have forbidden him to talk to anyone at the school again, and their anger at the school has also increased the risk of trusting school personnel. In short, implementing a relationship-based intervention would be inadvisable for Terrance at this point. Instead, interventions centered around responsibility can provide the predictability, safety, and consistency he craves—giving him something he can count on every day regardless of what else is happening in his life—without the risks that go along with depending on humans.

What additional information can we gather? We don't know enough about this situation. Let's gather some more information to see if we can build a plan that accurately and efficiently meets Terrance's needs. The following questions should launch our investigation. What other information would you like to gather?

- How does Terrance feel about the situation? Are Terrance and the school counselor still close, or did this upset ruin that relationship?
- Did anyone talk to Terrance's parents before the call to CPS was made? What was the school counselor's relationship with the parents? The principal's? Is there anyone in the building the parents

did connect positively with? Was this the first call to CPS, or have there been others?

• Did Terrance's behaviors escalate after the call took place, or did they stay about the same?

• When does Terrance tend to be the most disruptive? Is there a pattern? Are there certain times, days, or subjects that can be more triggering than others?

• Does Terrance have any siblings?

• Is there anyone in the school whom the parents aren't mad at? Is there anyone in the school who can connect positively with the parents?

Building Empathy and Exploring Terrance's Scenario from Five Perspectives

Now let's explore Terrance's scenario from the perspective of five stakeholders: the student, the parent/caregiver, the teacher, support staff, and the leader.

Student: My heart is hurting for Terrance, a 1st grader who lives in a home that has been unsafe and unpredictable. His downstairs brain is overdeveloped as a result of his living situation, and having to adapt to the structures of a school setting has most likely been rough for him. He probably struggles behaviorally because of his home life, and he has used his behaviors to let his teacher know that he is not OK. His teacher sent him to the school counselor, who was expected to "fix" Terrance so that he could learn better and not be so disruptive. Once they bonded, Terrance felt safe enough to disclose what was happening at home and ask for help, only to have that backfire on him. His sense of safety and trust is now compromised: both his parents and the school counselor seem unsafe and undependable. Even though the school counselor had an obligation to report his circumstances, that action hurt their relationship, and Terrance is now further isolated. Most likely, his destructive behaviors have worsened. He needs relationship, but he cannot trust it. It is crucial that this be addressed immediately.

Parent/caregiver: These parents are angry and upset. The school butted into their private lives and put their custody of their children at risk. They feel betrayed and unsafe and don't see a way they can partner with the school to help their son. As adults and as a couple, they are struggling, too—obviously, since they are using violence to manage their stress. The harmful effect on them and their children is significant. What must have happened in their own childhoods that led them to think hurting each other was a way to manage their stress? Parenting and providing a home for a family are challenging. Are the parents struggling financially? Besides violence, are they using other unhealthy coping strategies? Do they have anyone safe to turn to for help? Are they even able to see how their behavior toward each other may be affecting their son?

Teacher: I wonder what role the teacher is playing in this scenario. Clearly, she and Terrance's classmates are being affected by Terrance's behavior. Is this teacher involved in supporting Terrance, or has she solely relied on the school counselor to help Terrance during their weekly sessions? Does this teacher have the skill set to help Terrance, and some plans in place to help him regulate and be successful in the classroom?

Support staff/school counselor: I worry about the school counselor. I am wondering about the effect her mandatory call to CPS has had on her sense of self and her sense of competency. It is hard to have parents angry at us and even harder when they say hurtful and harmful things about us. The parents have also convinced their son that this counselor is not a safe person, defeating all the hard work she has done with Terrance. Is the counselor alone in this situation, or does she have the support of leadership and Terrance's teacher? Could the counselor have handled the situation differently?

Leader: What is the role of the leader in this situation? Is the principal aware of how angry these parents are and the effect it is having on Terrance, possibly his classmates, and the staff? What is the school's policy when it comes to mandated reporting? Is there a role that the principal can play in supporting the counselor and initiating repair with the parents? How involved is the principal (and others on the administrative team) with Terrance? What is their history, and how is their relationship?

Building a Plan to Support Terrance: Possible Interventions

For this scenario, I offer some alternatives to the tiered interventions we've discussed up to this point. Because we are all complex and have different experiences, I want to show a sampling of the multitude of options available for addressing student needs. In this case, we will focus on two things the school needs to do: initiate a repair with the family and create a plan to help Terrance.

Let's start with the repair. The school needs to make a sincere effort to mend fences and own its part of the rift with Terrance's parents. This will take longer than a meeting and needs to resonate deeper than words; the school will need to begin proving that it provides a safe place for Terrance and truly has Terrance's—and the family's—best interests at heart. Domestic violence is unequivocally not OK—*and* it is the reality for Terrance and his parents. They don't know how to do things differently at this point, and they are doing the best they can with the skill set they currently possess. There is *no* room for judgment. We've all worked with families whose parenting styles we didn't agree with, but fixating on the negative will yield only negative results. Instead, the goal is to connect with the family and (re)build a relationship so the positive can emerge. Based on my experience, I believe it would be best for the school administrator, Terrance's teacher, and the school counselor to sit down with the parents together for an initial repair-focused conversation.

If the parents opt to begin the conversation by sharing their frustrations, fears, hopes, or anger, then the school personnel's responsibility is simply to begin by *listening intently*—to truly hear the parents as they express their reality. Then it is the school's turn. I suggest using the six-step communication process I shared in *Fostering Resilient Learners:* listen, reassure, validate, respond, repair, resolve. The following is an example of what the principal might say to the family. See if you can note where and how the six communication steps are used here:

> Thank you for meeting with us. I know you are angry with the school, and your willingness to talk says a lot about your courage and your character. I know that we have upset you and that you may now see us as a threat to your family. I am sorry for that. We in no way intended to upset or offend you by making that call to CPS—and we did. I'm glad you're talking to us about this, because this is the only way we can all move past that and help Terrance.
>
> Terrance is an amazing young boy. [The principal describes his positive traits and perhaps a recent positive story.] We really like having him at this school, and we want him to be successful. That call to CPS compromised your sense of trust with us, and for that I am sorry. Our whole goal is to provide a safe place where students can learn and thrive, and we want Terrance to do just that. I am proud of Terrance because he had the courage to share things that

had him worried. Those worries were affecting his behavior and ability to learn.

We made that call because we are legally obligated to, and our mission is to protect our students. By making that call, we did not mean to imply that we think you don't love or care about Terrance. Obviously, you love and care for your son, or you wouldn't be meeting with us right now. I know it will take time for you to see that we really do want the best for Terrance, and it is our hope that we can heal from this and come together and find ways to help him be successful. We want to be a support to Terrance *and* to you. We recognize that the stress of raising a family can get overwhelming at times. We hope that we can meet with you regularly to help Terrance. We want to tell you about his awesomeness and his successes *and* access your expertise on how to help him when he is struggling. Would you be open and willing to do that?

The counselor must also repair with Terrance and get a feel for how they can safely continue to work together. She first needs to apologize for causing any stress to Terrance and assure him that the school is going to do its best to fix the situation. She should praise him for his courage in disclosing his difficult home situation and then work with him to come up with a plan to support him. What she should avoid is saying anything that leads Terrance to feel torn between the counselor and his parents. The goal of this intervention is to have Terrance feeling safe so he can do his job as a 1st grader: learn! Ideally, Terrance should believe the counselor is a safe person to whom he can confide his worries.

Keep in mind that Terrance is probably at risk for trusting other humans right now, so the school needs to design some plans that slowly reintroduce the possibility of connection, giving him predict-ability and something he can count on that has him wanting to come to school and feeling like he is safe and belongs there. The relation-ship strategy in Chapter 4 to "offer tangibles" would work well here. The counselor could give Terrance a worry stone that he can carry with him in his pocket. He can whisper his worries to the stone safely and keep it with him always. If his worries become too big and the stone gets "full," he can give the stone to his teacher, the counselor, or another adult in the school to let them know that things are super-hard and he needs their help. He can determine when the stone gets full and when he needs support, and he can pick whomever he wants to give the stone to so he or she can help him wash the worries away. This can serve as a signal to the adult that Terrance has a lot on his mind and his safety may be at risk, without putting pressure on Terrance to trust or confide in people at the school. The worry stone gives Terrance the control and permission to talk about his worries and seek help when he needs to.

Adding some specific responsibilities at both the school and the classroom level can also directly address Terrance's need for sta-bility and predictability and help him feel safe and connected.

A schoolwide intervention: Give Terrance a job. For instance, he could carry a box of books to the library every morning at a time that works with the daily schedule. This can also serve as a relational check-in opportunity that gets slowly introduced under the prem-ise that Terrance has a job to do. If Terrance is doing well, then he returns right away to class. If he is struggling that morning, the librar-ian can keep him there and have him do a few tasks, like shelving books or moving additional boxes—those weighted boxes actually promote regulation via proprioceptive input! Toward the end of the day, Terrance can return to the library and carry a box of books back to the classroom. This job gives Terrance something he can count on every day. His school role of official book carrier for his class provides an opportunity for a different relational connection, born from his special responsibility.

An in-classroom option: Terrance needs some responsibilities within the classroom as well. As Prince Praiser, his job during circle time is to sit in the chair above the other students on the carpet and be on the lookout for students who are on task and behaving well. He can have a special wand or sticker or star that denotes his role. Periodically throughout the lesson, the teacher can call on Prince Praiser to praise his fellow students' awesomeness.

The goal of this job is to give Terrance something that he can invest in and that builds his sense of self. When he believes he makes a valuable contribution to the school, he can grow. As he begins to trust the predictability and structure consistently provided by the school, he will begin to regulate more and will be less likely to have his downstairs brain driving his bus. Ideally, the repair process will help Terrance's parents, too, feel safe coming forward in support of Terrance, and with the regular positive communication from the school, they may begin to see alternative, healthier ways to manage their stress.

Support for the Staff of the Building

The principal, school counselor, and teacher need to reconnect on this case and help one another with a "reset." The reality is that Terrance may still be at risk despite their attempts to repair with the parents and provide an opportunity for them to manage their stress in different ways. Ideally, the parents will engage with the school and get the supports they need. But it is also possible that they will not, leaving the school staff feeling worried and sometimes helpless about how to protect Terrance.

Thus, these concerned personnel need to focus on what they can control, remembering that they are doing good things for kids and that their love and care are making a difference. They need to be reassured by one another that what they provide Terrance every day for six hours will make a difference in his life. And they need to be reminded not to give up or lose hope. This intervention is a marathon, not a sprint, and change will not occur overnight. Terrance will most likely have good days and not-so-good days. And although his parents may well be responsive to the school's repair attempts, it may take time for them to truly trust that outreach. The conversation between the school and the parents will most likely need to be repeated, and the principal and school counselor will need support from their fellow staff to be able to continue that dialogue. Seeing strength in others will help them manage this difficult situation. Putting check-in systems in place for involved staff members is essential, and giving them the opportunity to seek support and guidance whenever necessary will help them heal from this experience and not lose hope and motivation in their efforts to keep all kids safe.

Scenario #2 (Middle School): The Case of Kelsey

Kelsey is a middle school girl who has already been expelled from one school and is close to expulsion from another. She expects that the teachers will come to hate her, and she disrespects them verbally to speed up the process. She has begun walking out of class when she gets upset, which at her current school is usually grounds for automatic suspension.

What makes me think Kelsey requires a responsibility-based intervention? Kelsey is a perfect candidate for a responsibility-driven intervention because her systems of meaning have led her to believe that the school staff cannot possibly love or care about her. Her attempts at relationship have not worked well for her in the past, and as a result she is left with the mindset that people will eventually abandon her and kick her out. She appears to have a very negative sense of self. So, the school must attempt to engage Kelsey in a way that has her becoming self-reliant and believing that she is competent and capable of success.

What additional information can we gather? Here are some things I am wondering about:

- How long has Kelsey been at this new school, and how many times has she been suspended so far?
- Does she have friends at this school? Has she made any connections with an adult?
- What is the role of her family? Are they supportive, or are they disconnected from Kelsey's care?
- How do teachers and other staff talk about Kelsey in the staff lounge?
- Did the school take any proactive steps to support Kelsey and create a "fresh start" for her when she entered her new school?

Building Empathy and Exploring Kelsey's Scenario from Five Perspectives

Now let's explore Kelsey's scenario from the perspective of five stakeholders: the student, the parent/caregiver, the teacher, support staff, and the leader.

Student: I am concerned about Kelsey. This middle schooler with a developing brain has already had her systems of meaning impacted to the point that she believes she cannot be successful in school and teachers won't like her. So, she ruptures as a survival tactic, to avoid feeling hurt. In other words, she hurts others before they can hurt her. How lonely and isolated and misunderstood she must feel. She is also smart: she has learned quickly how to avoid relationship and to make people angry, even though she craves connection. To her, it feels safer to avoid relationship than to risk being hurt. What experiences have led her to become so guarded at such a young age?

Parent/caregiver: It's hard to fill in this piece because we are unsure of the role Kelsey's parents play in her life. I am not sure whom she lives with. We can guess that if Kelsey has been expelled from other schools, her parents' trust in schools may be marginal, at best. I would be concerned that they wouldn't believe in school as a source of support for their daughter and that they might avoid calls home because of Kelsey's history of disruption. How can the school align with her caregivers to show them that here, Kelsey will get real support?

Teacher: This is rough for Kelsey's teachers. No one likes to be sworn at or verbally disrespected. It is hard to want to build a relationship with a student who says hurtful things and avoids learning. Teachers' motivation to connect with a student who behaves in that manner is already minimal, and if her behavior disrupts others, it can throw her teachers off for the entire day. Because she is new to the school and has a history of expulsion, some teachers may already be expecting her to be gone before long; some may even be thinking, "Good riddance." But where is the empathy in that? If we allow ourselves to admit that we do feel that way, how does that affect our sense of self and our faith in ourselves as good stewards of this profession?

Support staff: How many people—including adults—has Kelsey reamed out when crossing paths with them at school? The list could be long. The challenges Kelsey's teachers face are probably prevalent throughout campus.

Leader: The work is cut out for this leader, too. Not only must she address the behaviors of a new student, but she also has to manage the emotions of the staff. How do you instill a sense of motivation and desire to help a young student with a history like Kelsey's? How many other students is this leader dealing with who are presenting the same issues? How can we remember to have empathy for a leader who must balance such challenges? And how can we empower her to help motivate the student and the staff to do anything differently?

Building a Plan to Support Kelsey: Possible Interventions

In this scenario, we've identified Kelsey as a very high-risk young lady, so we're going to suggest the following possible Tier 3 interventions to provide her with the most consistent, intense support possible. Ideally, as Kelsey's trust and connection to the school grow, the intensity of these suggested interventions would decrease.

Kelsey's whole system of meaning has led her to believe that she cannot be successful. It's not at all surprising that she doesn't trust relationship at this point because the adults in her world have shown her that she isn't worth fighting for and that she is easy to abandon. She has learned to affirm that way of thinking through the behavior choices she makes. The school's goal is to get her invested and able to see herself as an important part of something good. Everyone involved must find a way to engage her so that she can begin to open her mind to the possibility that she is capable of learning and being a successful student.

Kelsey is a prime example of a student who needs the adults in her life to be on the same page. She has triggered a number of adults in the building, and I'm assuming that their views of Kelsey are not positive. So, this problem cannot be left to just one person to solve. Kelsey's case illustrates why we need to view all students in a school as *our* students. Years of not-OK experiences have led to this predicament, and the school community must unite to move Kelsey and the staff toward success. Kelsey is capable of awesomeness, and by working together, stakeholders can put a team plan in place to help actualize this outcome.

Kelsey's support team should include teachers who have Kelsey in class, the school counselor, a member of leadership, a support staff member, Kelsey, and her parents or caregivers. Everyone, including Kelsey, is responsible for improving this situation. The goal is to give Kelsey a different vision—to give her something she can count on, be a part of, and have some control over. The following are some examples of ways to reach out to and support Kelsey. These interventions would fall to various team members depending on their roles, skill sets, available time, comfort level, and relationships with Kelsey.

- *Call home.* Talk with the parents and learn about Kelsey. What does she like? What is she into? How does she spend her time? Welcome them to the school, showing genuine interest in their daughter, and let them know that you want to work with them for Kelsey's sake, and you are going to fight to keep her in school because your school is where she belongs.
- *Meet with Kelsey.* Welcome Kelsey, letting her know that you are aware of her history and you want things to be different for her here. You want her to come to school, stay in school, and be successful in school.
- *Talk to the teachers.* Remind teachers that Kelsey's behavior isn't personal or about them; rather, it is her way of protecting herself

against being hurt, and it is all she knows how to do. Talk to them about how they can start the class differently with Kelsey—for example, by giving her jobs or tasks to focus on so she doesn't have to act out. Give them permission to let her take breaks to get a drink of water, use the restroom, or visit a trusted adult.

• *Reconsider the suspension rule.* Isn't storming out of class actually better than blowing up in class? Can you put a plan in place so that when Kelsey feels herself start to burst, she signals the teacher that she needs a break and then has permission to go to certain designated areas to get back into the learning mode?

• *Let Kelsey know that leaving your school is not an option.* Negotiate with Kelsey. Give her some autonomy; odds are, she doesn't have much control in her life. Cede some control over her learning and see what she thinks she needs. If she weren't getting suspended and actually liked school, what would that look like?

• *Conduct a reset.* This is a job for the principal. Meet with Kelsey and explain that you want to meet with her every day and learn how things are going. You are assigning her the job of helping you make the school better; she's your agent in the field. She will report what she thinks will make the school awesome. As someone who has attended multiple middle schools, her insight is valuable. What does this school need to do to make kids want to stay and learn? She can use her prior experiences to add perspective and invest in making this school—*her* school—great!

Scenario #3 (High School): The Case of Paul

Paul is a junior in high school who recently experienced a trauma that has caused him to distrust females. If he interacts with an adult female, he will act out or leave class entirely.

What makes me think Paul requires a responsibility-based intervention? OK, detectives, let's get working on this case. Paul has been wounded by an adult, and his sense of faith and trust in adults, especially women, has been compromised. We don't know the details, but we can assume there's legitimacy to his position. Therefore, putting together interventions around responsibility will minimize the likelihood that Paul will be triggered in the presence of an adult female. His sense of self and his ability to trust have been affected. The school can help him reinstill his sense of self in a positive way, giving him something he can rely on—something not based on human response.

What additional information can we gather? There are a lot of unanswered questions surrounding Paul's scenario. Here are a few questions I have right off the bat:

• How recent is this trauma? Is Paul receiving the time and grace he needs to heal, or are school personnel forcing relationship on him when he is still very fragile?

• Has Paul had a history of acting out? Is this new behavior resulting from the trauma, or did the trauma exacerbate existing behaviors?

• Who in the school is safe for Paul?

• Are there any adult females Paul does not act out with or escape from?

• Where does Paul go when he leaves class?

Building Empathy and Exploring Paul's Scenario from Five Perspectives

Now let's explore Paul's scenario from the perspective of five stakeholders: the student, the parent/caregiver, the teacher, support staff, and the leader.

Student: Paul experienced a trauma that had a significant effect on his sense of safety. His system of meaning is strong—so strong that he currently cannot distinguish a real from a perceived threat when he sees an adult female. Because of this, all adult females are unsafe. He is relying on this strong mindset to keep himself safe. School staff need to be mindful of this.

Parent/caregiver: I am unsure if the trauma stemmed from the actions of a parent or someone known to the parents, or whether the parents are supportive of Paul and what he has gone through. Depending on the answers, Paul's parents likely need support, too. If they are not the cause of the trauma, do they even know that Paul has experienced this not-OK event? If they do know, they must be worried about their son and concerned about how he is managing this experience. They need support and reassurance, and they must be included in Paul's intervention plan.

Teacher: Female teachers should beware: their mere presence is a threat to Paul, so they must be cautious. Reassuring Paul that they are safe will not honor Paul but, instead, cause further harm. A female teacher's need to reassure him does not align with *his* need to protect himself right now. Male teachers have a huge task here: they aren't just the safe option for Paul, but they are also faced with slowly giving Paul permission to feel safe at school and with all the teachers, including the females. This is a difficult spot for Paul's teachers to be in.

Support staff, especially counselor(s): Support staff will need to advocate for Paul right now, helping the teachers see that his behaviors are not personal, but merely his attempt to feel safe. They may need to get creative with his schedule for a while. Junior year can be a brutal year, and no one wants Paul to fall further behind than he already has. These staff members need to work in partnership with their team to help Paul heal from this experience.

Leader: The leader should keep his eyes and ears open to ensure that Paul's privacy is being respected and that the staff is mindful of how much he is suffering. He can reassure teachers that this isn't personal and that if this were their son, the leader would want the school to have a sensitive and supportive plan in place. The leader also has leverage to adapt Paul's schedule, modify activities, and run interference between Paul and any adult females with whom he might interact.

Building a Plan to Support Paul: Possible Interventions

Whether we consider our interventions for Paul to be Tier 2 (short-term and proactive) or Tier 3 (more intensive), it's time to rally the team. Supporting a student in a rough patch like Paul is not something any individual can do alone. This is a great opportunity to form a support team to help Paul regain trust and return to the learning mode. This team can meet and identify who would best support Paul through this difficult time. Paul should be a part of this process; his consent and participation are crucial for reestablishing trust. The following are some examples of ways to reach out to and support Paul.

• *Meet with Paul.* A safe adult in the building whom Paul can trust should meet with Paul and, ideally, his parents or a close friend. This adult should reinforce that he is sensitive to what Paul is going through and that Paul needs to stay in school and learn, and then ask Paul what he needs to get through this experience. The adult can then explore options with Paul, such as

– A temporary schedule change where he has only male teachers.

– An opportunity to do independent work in the classes led by female teachers. This is ideal because it honors Paul's need to feel safe and still allows him to stay on his schedule and be accountable for his work. He can e-mail assignments and begin to engage in exchanges with his female teachers at a safe distance. This can lead to meeting with the teacher and another adult or student of his choice to review the learning and, eventually, make a full return to class.

– Identification of safe places on campus for Paul to work, complete his assignments, study, and interact with other safe adults.

• *Set aside time and space for breaks.* The team can put a plan in place that allows Paul to take a break without disrupting or saying hurtful things to others in the school. Paul's safe adult can validate that his feelings are real and may be overpowering at times, and ask Paul how he could communicate his needs to the adults in the building.

• *Broaden Paul's perspective.* Once the team has put supports for Paul's safe functioning in place, it can support him in gradually opening his mindset, giving him permission not to see all adult women as threats. When Paul is stable, he can be incrementally exposed to safe, supportive female adults in the building.

• *Reevaluate Paul's plan every two to three weeks.* The team should slowly work Paul back toward his original schedule, making sure to include him in this process. He needs to be invested in the goal of this plan and his learning and to see that school is a safe place for him.

In cases like these, it's important that we be flexible in meeting our students' needs. Life is messy and unpredictable, and our goal is establishing and maintaining a safe environment for our students so that they can learn and thrive. Sometimes, making temporary adjustments, bending the rules, lifting some restrictions, and enacting small changes are worth the effort because the result is far better than the trauma that could result from our rigidity and lack of flexibility. When we're all truly committed to our fragile students like Paul, we're much more likely to help them recover quickly and safely.

....

Conclusion

The goal of this chapter is to provide a variety of creative ways for addressing student need through responsibility-based interventions. These difficult scenarios gave me the opportunity to introduce positive ways of reframing supports as well as acknowledging the need for repair, even while fulfilling our civic and legal duties to protect children. I wanted to highlight how we need to come together and address our most challenging situations from a "we" standpoint. We share all our students, and we share responsibility for each and every one of them—together.

In the schools I have worked in, we have formed "we caught you" teams intended to support staff and students alike through difficult times. The concept behind the teams is "We're here for you, no matter what!" These teams are intended to provide positive and time-limited support in response to students and staff who are dealing with the messiness of life. Remember, trauma is nondiscriminatory: it hits us all, and often without warning. So let's band together and remember that we're all human, and we're all travelers on this journey together. Life is hard, and sometimes we're going through some muck that requires a little extra assistance, patience, support, interventions, and, yes: grace.

6

Regulation

Be cool.

—The Fonz

....

Although regulation is the last of the new three *R*s I present in this book, it is perhaps the most essential. After all, regulation is the targeted outcome of the other two *R*s: we build and tend to *relationship* to help our students achieve regulated states, and we offer opportunities to develop *responsibility* to help our students self-regulate.

Regulation: *the ability to take in stimuli and manage emotional and behavioral responses accordingly. Regulated students can access reason in their upstairs brain.*

Fortunately for us as professionals, regulation is also the most basic, least complicated intervention we can provide. That doesn't mean it's easy to help students regulate but, rather, that it's a direct *A*-to-*B*, cause-and-effect connection we're trying to make.

The easiest way to think of regulation is to connect it back to our discussion of the upstairs and downstairs brain in Chapter 2. When we are in our upstairs brain, we're regulated, under control, and rational. This is the place where we can access all the skills and capacities that enable us to make healthy choices. The downstairs brain, by contrast, houses our flight-fight-freeze response. It's that dark spot we find ourselves in moments of stress, uncertainty, anxiety, or fear. We know what happens to our capacity to learn when our regulation is compromised and we're in our downstairs brain. Simply put, we must be regulated to learn.

Our goal is to get into—and stay in—our upstairs brain.

It All Starts in Our Brains

Every day, we are learning more about the brain and its capacity. Amazing researchers, scientists, doctors, and authors like John Medina, Judy Willis, Bruce Perry, Sheryl Feinstein, and Dan Siegel, among many others, have helped us make sense of the brain so we can teach it to others—including our students. The overarching goal of a regulation-based intervention is to provide students with the skills and capacity to regulate their bodies so they stay in the learning mode, releasing healthy chemicals—dopamine, serotonin, endorphins—conducive to brain growth and development.

If we look at the brain from a regulation standpoint, we can design interventions that will help our students stay in their upstairs brain or return to it when they become dysregulated. Further, if we can teach our students to recognize and attune to their own biology, they can signal us when they are moving away from learning and headed toward their downstairs brain. When a brain feels safe, it produces chemicals that allow it to develop and stay in its higher-functioning part (upstairs brain). When the brain senses threat or feels unsafe, it releases chemicals that move it to the survival area (downstairs brain). The chronic release of those survival chemicals, like cortisol and adrenaline, can be toxic to the brain and the body and severely disrupt healthy growth and development.

Our brains were wired to survive—not thrive.

When we start to look at behavior through this lens, we tend to build more empathy, realizing that the behavior happening in front of us may be a "can't" issue rather than a "won't" issue. If we remind ourselves that students' brains are behaving exactly as they have been wired to do, then we can start to put together a plan to support healthy regulation. When we start to shift our mindset from "What is wrong with this kid?" to "What has happened to this kid?" we can enhance our empathy even further. This empathy will remind us that Alicia is doing the best she can with what she's got, and that we must partner with Dawson to help him manage his stress. All our students need us to focus on their strengths and potential. They look to us to provide assurance that we see them as having potential in a safe, predictable, and consistent manner.

Pete's Practice

Biologically, our brains are amazing. I don't think anyone would dispute that. Words like *nuance*, *variation*, and *interpretation* were all created to describe the ways our brain takes information and analyzes the subtleties that distinguish different situations, colors, facial expressions, memories—you name it. The brain is one cool in-skull supercomputer.

And, as our central processor, the brain is very helpful. Think of it in these terms: as humans out in the natural world, we're really prey animals. So when we're gathering berries out in the woods and we're confronted by a bear, we *need* our downstairs brain to kick in. The chemicals released—cortisol and adrenaline—give us a shot of strength, clarity of purpose, and drive. We immediately enter survival mode: flight, fight, or freeze. We run away from danger (in this case, the bear). When we're cornered or cannot run anymore, we turn and fight. And yes, there are times when our fear renders us incapable of responding, so we freeze: *Is this the "make loud noises" bear or the "curl up into the fetal position" bear?*

Note that these hairy interactions with bears and other threats are not intended to be lengthy. The chemicals our brain authorizes for immediate release are designed to be quick-acting, staying in our system just long enough for us to escape and find safety. For those purposes, they're incredibly helpful.

However, students who live in trauma, who have experienced complex trauma, or whose trauma history generates that sickening anticipation of the not-OK are continuously exposed to those chemicals, which can be toxic to their bodies. These chemicals stifle the production of healthy, upstairs-brain chemicals and wreak havoc on the body's normal, everyday systems.

At one of the schools where I was principal, we had a 1st grader (I'll call him Abraham) who lived in such a chaotic and scary household that he was on edge every moment. That mentality carried into the schoolhouse, too. It was painful to watch him constantly twitch his head to be sure nothing (or nobody) was sneaking up on him. He reacted to his teachers' directions, other staff members' requests, and his classmates' interactions defensively and aggressively, often escalating innocuous situations into full-blown confrontations.

We partnered Abraham with a young instructional assistant in our school named Tom. After weeks of saying "hello" to Abraham, visiting his classroom, and playing soccer with him on the field, Tom forged a bond with Abraham. Whenever Abraham's behaviors escalated beyond his teacher's influence, we would call Tom on the walkie-talkie, and he would escort Abraham out of the classroom.

Once outside, they would go for a walk, stop to get a drink of water, visit the campus garden, straighten out the bulletin boards in the hallway, count the different-colored cars in the school parking lot, and so on. Whatever they did, it helped Abraham get back to his upstairs brain, process what happened and discuss strategies with Tom, and return to the business of learning. These regulating activities also allowed Tom to help Abraham understand that he was safer at school than he thought he was.

We aren't supposed to be chased by bears all the time. Creating opportunities to regulate—to get back into the upstairs brain—allows for the normal and safe distribution of chemicals in our bodies.

Although we can't necessarily prevent trauma from happening, we can give students tools to manage the stress associated with it. When we address regulation needs, we provide our students with the skills to manage their stress in healthy ways.

In my consulting work throughout the United States, I am frequently called the "Brain Lady" because I believe strongly in teaching about the brain and using this as a powerful universal communication tool with our students and families. When we can understand our body's biology and reaction to stress, we can better equip ourselves to manage it in healthy ways. I credit Dr. Dan Siegel at UCLA for this insight, especially his saying, "If we can name it, then we can tame it." That is what we are trying to empower our students to do.

Check out Dr. Siegel's "Hand Model of the Brain" video on YouTube: https://www.youtube.com/watch?v=gm9CIJ74Oxw

I have taught about the brain to students, teachers, parents, administrators, counselors, and other educators and caregivers in every role and context. I firmly believe that this is *the thing* that could unite us with a common language, transforming the way we view, understand, and communicate about behaviors. I've seen firsthand how gaining this understanding has transformed schools. Parents have shared their hope that they and their children can learn to control their bodies and manage their stress. Staff appreciate being able to reconcile their faith and belief in their kids with their negative perceptions that sometimes result from their students' misbehavior. And I've had students come up to me and say, "Brain Lady, I'm not just in my downstairs brain—I'm in my shoes!"

As we attune to ourselves, we can start to manage what's happening in our brains and our bodies intentionally. And as professionals, we know to respond to students in their downstairs brains with "What do you think you need to get back upstairs so you can learn?" The "upstairs brain/downstairs brain" language meshes well with social-emotional learning (SEL) programs that schools and districts are already implementing. How amazing would it be if our entire education system used this language to promote regulation? If every student in every school knew what *upstairs brain* and *downstairs brain* meant and could use this language to get the support and tools they need to regulate?

I'd like to share a story to illustrate the power of this common approach. When I was working at Washington State University in the Child and Family Research Unit for CLEAR, my colleague and I were assigned to support schools in different parts of a state. We were both known as the Brain Ladies in our respective schools, and we taught the brain language to staff members and students during our monthly visits over the course of several years.

Once when I was in one of my schools, I came across a young boy who was sitting, sad and alone, in the hallway. He was new to the school, having just been moved within the foster-care system to a new family. As I talked to him, I learned that he had come from a school at which my colleague was working. It turned out he knew his Brain Lady well, so I sought to build a connection by asking, "Do you know that I'm the Brain Lady in this school?" Eyes wide, he replied, "Really?" I told him that his Brain Lady and I were good friends, at which point his frown transformed into a giant smile. I then asked, "Would you like to call your Brain Lady? We could FaceTime with her." He grinned even wider and nodded his head. When the two connected through my phone, I'm not sure which one was happier; they had obviously forged a strong mutual bond. After a few minutes of talking, this boy was able to return to a regulated state and enter his classroom to learn.

I cannot overemphasize what a difference this connection made for this young boy, who had been moved from home to home and city to city, experiencing more not-OK than anyone should have to. His sense of safety, his sense of trust, and his need for relationship were chronically being compromised. But just knowing that his new school had a Brain Lady too had a significant effect on his ability to regulate, his sense of self, and his willingness to take the risk of trusting yet another set of providers. I will forever remember that moment and will continue to encourage all schools to unite around this common language.

How Can We Tell If a Student Has an Unmet Regulation Need?

Typically, students who struggle with regulation are the ones who cause adults the most angst, as they often contribute to the disruption of the learning environment. Keep in mind that many of our students present with a combination of needs, and no matter what the needs are, regulation management is a skill we can all benefit from learning.

Attuning to our biological signals and adopting skills that help us return to a regulated state are essential components to successful learning and living. In my experience, there are several behavioral expressions that might correlate with a need to develop regulation skills. A student with such a need may . . .

• *Have a tough time with transitions.* Transitions can trigger almost any student, and students who struggle with regulation are particularly susceptible. Shifting from one activity to another, changing from one class to another, or moving from one place in the room to another can be a cause of stress or anxiety. Any change—including substitute teachers, schedule disruptions, assemblies, and even announcements over the PA system—can be difficult to manage.

• *Fidget constantly.* We know these students; their continual movement makes them conspicuous. Such wiggly worms may struggle to sit still, remain in their assigned spot, attend to the task, or focus on their work. Because of this tendency to get distracted and shuffle around, they may also be quick to become agitated—or agitate the adults and students nearby.

• *Shut down.* Sometimes, students who are in a stressed, dysregulated state access the "freeze" part of their downstairs brain and close themselves off from everyone around them. This could be manifested by hiding under a desk or table, wrapping a hoodie over their heads, putting up a proverbial wall of disinterest, or daydreaming.

• *Flip his or her lid suddenly.* Have you ever had a student drop into his or her downstairs brain for a reason you couldn't fathom? Often, these episodes appear to us as dramatic overreactions when we're regulated and in our upstairs brains. For students who struggle with self-regulation, the slightest incident might trigger an emotional response.

- *Be on an emotional roller coaster.* We've all had interactions with students when we didn't know what to expect. Will this comment trigger the student, or will it be OK? What kind of response will we get after announcing this decision? Sometimes we're met with excitement and joy, other times with irritation and anger. Wide fluctuations in emotional response are often an indication of the need to provide regulation supports.

Universal Trauma-Invested Regulation-Establishing Strategies

First and foremost, when you start to incorporate regulation strategies and tools into your setting, do not attempt anything that will send *you* to *your* downstairs brain. Just because a colleague has opted to replace all her chairs with exercise balls does not mean you need to do it if you know it will drive you crazy. You can only provide what you know you can handle, because if you aren't regulated, your students won't be, either. So give yourself some grace. Start slow, try things that you think will work, and partner with your students to help identify what you can all consent and commit to. The key with any tool or strategy we use is the way we communicate its purpose. When we explain *why* we are introducing this tool, students can comprehend its value and are more likely to comply with its use. I cannot overstate the importance of consent: we set the tone for investing in learning together, creating a culture in which we're all willing to "give it a shot."

I might introduce regulation tools like this:

> Hi, team. I have some tools and ideas that I have brought to class with me that are designed to help your brains get in learning-ready states. Your job when you come to school is to learn, and sometimes we have stuff going on in our lives that

makes it harder for us to focus and learn. We might be worried about something. We might be hungry or tired. We might have seen or experienced something that has upset or hurt us. Whatever the reason, I get that sometimes learning is hard. I also get that all our brains are different. Sometimes our brains need more support, and sometimes there are certain subjects or topics that make it harder for us to focus. My goal is to help you learn despite those potential struggles.

So, I have come up with a bunch of ideas and tools that you can access that may help you better be able to learn. Keep in mind that I need to see evidence that this tool is truly helping you learn and that you are focused and improving. If I see that this tool is causing you to be even more distracted and off task, then clearly it is not a tool—it is more of a toy, and now is not the time to play with toys. These tools can't distract your teammates or me, either. So, if you feel like your brain needs additional support, I want you to signal to me that you need some help. With my permission, you can access a tool that you think may help you. We will work together to ensure that the tool is serving its purpose. You may only need the tool for a few minutes to get back on track, or you may need it more regularly for support. Do you think we can work as a team to do this? We must all work together to be the best learners we can be.

The following are examples of regulation strategies and tools that I've seen work effectively in various settings.

1. **Provide a weighted pencil.** Kids who have a hard time regulating often struggle with fine motor skills. Use of weights on a pen or pencil helps the body move back into a regulated state, as the heft

reminds the child that there is something in his or her hand. Not only does this strategy help calm the nerves, but it might even improve your student's handwriting.

2. **Provide a weighted lap pad.** Students who need a boost with attention or calming might benefit from a weighted lap pad. This is simply a heavier-than-normal blanket, pillow, or stuffed animal that can rest on a child's lap and aid with regulation and soothing.

3. **Play soothing music.** Music can set the tone in an environment—think about the kind of music you play in your headphones when you commute or work out. The same holds true for a classroom. By attending to the music you play in the background, you can reinforce the mood that best matches the needs of the students, the task, and the climate you're attempting to establish.

4. **Offer a stress ball or a worry stone.** This is something tangible that students can use to help them focus and regulate; it doesn't need to be a stress ball or a worry stone specifically. The mere rubbing or touch of this item offers *proprioceptive* input, promoting awareness and giving students permission to regulate their bodies.

Proprioception: **the awareness of stimuli and the ability to sense one's own body location in its physical space.**

5. **Play catch.** Sometimes, students can develop hand-eye coordination and reduce stress simultaneously. By gently tossing and catching a small beanbag, foam ball, or mini-pillow in front of them, they can focus their brains on a soft, harmless, quiet task. Like all the options listed here, this would need to be practiced under adult supervision, and expectations would need to be spelled out very clearly.

6. **Let students choose where to work.** This strategy, which appeared in Chapter 5, works just as well for building regulation as

it does for developing responsibility. Give students permission to pick a spot in the room where they know they can learn successfully and their upstairs brains will be in charge. You'll know students have identified productive spots when you see them successfully engaged in learning.

I was working in a school with a student who clearly struggled to remain in his upstairs brain. He was a busy boy and did not function well being confined to his desk; he learned much better when he could lie on the floor and write using a clipboard. His teacher struggled with this, believing that permitting him to lie on the floor meant she was giving up her power over the student and the class. When we talked about it from a regulation standpoint and discussed how she could explain the purpose of the strategy and set clear expectations for students, she agreed to give it a try. The effect was transformational. The student did attempt in the beginning to push the boundaries by rolling back and forth, but the teacher was able to reset him by reminding him of the expectations for this strategy's use. Once that boundary was restated and enforced, the student thrived from this accommodation. His focus increased, his schoolwork improved, and the teacher's perceptions of him improved, too.

Sometimes the value of a choice that will promote success outweighs the need for perceived control over a setting. By allowing some flexibility, this teacher actually gained more control of the class and its success than she ever did from engaging in the daily power struggle to get this student to sit still at his desk.

7. **Keep students' hands busy.** Allowing students to doodle, draw, or knit at their desks while listening can boost regulation. Sometimes distracting our hands focuses our brains. I have provided countless professional development trainings through which adults crochet, sketch, and scribble, allowing their brains to engage in the executive

functions of concentrating and analyzing information. Your students may need this as a source of support as well.

8. **Offer brain breaks.** Our brains were not wired to function or focus for more than a few minutes at a time. The longer we sit, the harder it is to focus and keep on track. Conventional wisdom advises us to limit the time we engage kids in a single activity structure to one minute for each year of the children's age. So, 5-year-olds can engage for five minutes, 6-year-olds for six minutes, and so forth, before they need a brain break. Providing brain breaks like the examples that follow can help students maintain focus and remember content more efficiently.

- *Calisthenics:* Jumping jacks, air squats, pushups, running in place, and other quick exercises can help get the blood pumping again.
- *Yoga or Pilates:* These exercises tend to require an exertion of mental focus that connects with the body, building proprioceptive awareness.
- *Thumb wrestling or rock-paper-scissors tourney:* How cool would it be to have an in-class tournament? When a student wins, the opponent stands behind the victor and cheers during the next competition. This continues until the class crowns the only undefeated champion.
- *Standing up or sitting down:* Depending on which students *were* doing, swap 'em!
- *Moving around the room:* Read the walls, engage in a scavenger hunt, or just walk for 100 steps. For additional spirit, move around the room in a conga line!
- *Switching seats:* Moving to a new spot engages new parts of the brain to acclimate to the fresh surroundings.

• *Talking to an elbow partner:* Asking students to talk briefly to the neighbor whose elbow is closest to their own provides a brain break and can also be a way to check for understanding as students process information or examine their answers to a question.

• *Cross-lateral exercises:* Touching the elbow to the opposite knee, doing opposite-toe touches, "dabbing," kicking legs at a diagonal, and other quick exercises that force limbs to cross the midline—that imaginary line dividing the left side of the body from the right—help activate both hemispheres of the brain during a lesson, when usually only one is firing.

• *Meditation or mindfulness practice:* Usually accompanied by a heightened awareness of one's breathing, one's body, and one's thoughts, these practices encourage a level of tranquility that most teachers dream of—so why not aim for it?

• *Drinking some water:* We know the brain needs water to survive and thrive, so a quick break to fulfill this basic need can be a lifesaver for students to regulate. An added benefit is the walk required to go to the drinking fountain. If a student is particularly squirmy, perhaps a pass to use the drinking fountain at the far end of the hallway is in order.

Scenarios for Us to Process Together

In the following pages, I share three real scenarios—one at the elementary school level, one at the middle school level, and one at the high school level—for us to investigate together. We will make observations, analyze root causes, ask follow-up questions, and form hypotheses. To help you process and act on similar scenarios you face in your work, I add my own two cents with a series of possible interventions focused on helping students self-regulate—and *remain* regulated.

Scenario #1 (Elementary School):
A Classroom in Chaos

A teacher describes her situation:

> I'm having an issue with multiple students who have impulse
> control issues that are really disruptive to the entire class. I'm
> struggling with how to keep them in class without compro-
> mising the entire room's education.

I'm guessing that this scenario may resonate with you. I hear about this situation all the time from amazing educators across the board: newbies and veterans, teachers in public and private schools, teachers across all demographics—you name it. This isn't just an elementary school conundrum, either. This teacher is asking a universal question: how do I avoid using the exit strategy for a few students while still meeting the needs of all? Let's see if we can identify a few ways to help with this.

But first, I have a favor to ask: Because this scenario may be triggering for you, please make sure that as you read on, you are staying in your upstairs brain. Take some deep breaths, grab a stress ball, cross the midline if you have to, and open up your mind to some possibilities. The following foundational beliefs must ring true for you before you continue:

- All kids deserve an education.
- Every kid has potential.
- Each and every one of your students has strengths.

- You are amazing and dedicated to doing the best you can for your students, and your job is not always easy.
- Everyone deserves grace.

What makes me think the students in this class would benefit from a regulation-based intervention? The phrase used to describe this situation is "students who have impulse control issues." To me, this indicates that these students are having a tough time with regulation and staying in their upstairs brains. They are struggling with body control and are sending a message that they could use some help to gain control in nondistracting ways.

What additional information can we gather? Let's gather some more information. The following questions should launch our investigation.

- What does "multiple students" mean? Exactly how many students are we talking about? Is this most of the class or a select few students?
- If the issue is prevalent with most of the class, might that indicate a classroom management issue? Does the teacher need mentoring and support to gain skills and confidence in meeting her students' needs so they don't have to disrupt class to get their needs met?
- Is this a new teacher or a seasoned teacher? A motivated teacher or a burned-out teacher?
- When the students disrupt, what does it look like? Is it a safety issue, or is it just annoying?
- Does this teacher have any support from the administration, a mentor, teammates, or anyone else in the building?
- Do these tough nuggets have additional support? Are they on the school's radar, or are they newly emerging concerns to the staff?

- What systems of meaning is the teacher accessing? Is this "that class"? Are these students whom the teacher was warned about beforehand? Does the teacher believe she has been given a rough group this year?
- What interventions have been tried? What has worked? What hasn't? For which students did each specific intervention work (or not), and to what extent? Let's get detailed.

Building Empathy and Exploring This Classroom Scenario from Five Perspectives

Now let's explore this scenario from the perspective of five stakeholders: the student, the parent/caregiver, the teacher, support staff, and the leader.

Student: Clearly, these students are struggling to find healthy ways to stay regulated. How overwhelmed they must feel, not knowing how to manage their bodies effectively. Are they feeding off one another in negative instead of positive ways, in the sense that misery loves company? Are their systems of meaning developing in such a way that their goal is to avoid learning and to act out when things get tough? Who sees these students as people with strength and potential? What would that look like? How might they respond to this? When was the last time they thought something positive about themselves? When were they last excited to go home and share that they had a great day?

Parent/caregiver: I wonder if the caregivers for these children have united in their frustration to rally against the school, seeing this as part of a larger problem. Or is each family feeling isolated and alone, dreading the call from the school saying yet again what isn't working with their child? Are the caregivers struggling with their child's behavior, or are they so overwhelmed by their own stresses that they have no idea their child is truly in trouble? Are they known to the school as "those kids' parents," or are they overlooked because they have been avoiding contact and connection? What must be happening in their minds when they think about the well-being of their child?

Teacher: I just want to give this teacher a hug. How many of us have had years when our classes were challenging, when the number of tough nuggets outweighed the "easy" students? Just thinking about it makes me feel exhausted. Maybe this teacher never got to learn about classroom management and is fumbling in the dark, wanting desperately to do right by her students but not knowing how. Maybe she is realizing the overwhelming needs of her students and is aware of the many stressors they carry with them that affect their capacity to learn and to focus. How can her team validate for her that this is a tough situation—and that she can make a difference? How can she be empowered to feel supported and less alone in this venture?

Support staff: If this handful (or more) of students is disruptive in the classroom, what must they be like in the hallways, in the cafeteria, in the gym, on the playground, on the bus, and in other common areas? What is the support staff experiencing? Are the same students struggling to get into the learning mode all day long, or are there some contexts where various students can regulate successfully? How are the support staff members handling this? Are they looking for strengths, or waiting for the kids to disrupt and get ejected? Do staff members play roshambo for the "privilege" of accompanying students in the classrooms or other settings? Is anyone asking members of the support staff if they're having success with some of the tough nuggets and, if so, whether they could share that success with others? And what of the school counselor? Does the counseling office become the island to which students are exiled to be "fixed"?

Leader: What does the relationship between the leader and the teacher look like? Does the teacher feel safe enough to approach her boss for support? Are they stuck in admiring the problem, or are they working collectively toward finding a solution? I am concerned about this leader. How many of her teachers are facing similar problems—struggling to avoid the exit strategy and simultaneously asserting that things are "out of control"? Do staff members blame the leader for this state of affairs? Is she facing policies and legislation that demand results, which requires teachers to keep their students yet fails to provide them with the skills and resources necessary to help them?

Building a Plan to Support This Class: Possible Interventions

In this section, I offer possible classroom interventions at three tiers, moving from broader to more targeted tactics, followed by more targeted interventions for each of our five stakeholder groups.

Tier 1: The first thing that comes to my mind in this scenario is the idea of routines and rituals. What predictable measures and routines can this teacher put in place to support whole-class regulation? How can she put her students on track to get back to their upstairs brains? Let's give this educator permission to sit her class down and have a "do over." She might start by saying the following to her class:

> OK, everyone, for some reason our team has gotten *way* off track, and we're losing precious learning time as a result. I know I'm feeling some frustration at how things are going, and I'm sure you all are, too. We need to work together as a

team to get back on track. I'm sorry that we've lost our way, and I'm sad that our team has become so distracted. So, I propose that we have a reset and start over! From now on, we are going to put some new rituals and rules in place to help us get as learning-ready as possible.

Then she could pick one or two routines to implement with her whole class. (Any more than that, and she may become overwhelmed and be at further risk for burnout.) For example, one new routine could be singing a song to start the day, to mark transitions between subjects and breaks, and to close the day. Another routine could be a hand signal the teacher asks students to use to check in throughout the day, with a closed fist signifying upstairs brain, or learning-ready; a *C*-shaped hand meaning learning-compromised and in need of a quick reset; and an open hand signifying downstairs brain. In the last case, the whole class may need a brain break or a reset. Keep in mind that depending on the class, losing 20 percent of students to their downstairs brains is a good indicator for us to provide a reset opportunity.

Shifting some practices for the entire class can be a very effective first step. New routines force students to attend to the directions and the details of the changes and to absorb what it will take to meet the expectations. I'm not advocating for a complete overhaul, but a couple of new brain tools or brain breaks that the teacher can commit to, focus on, and explain clearly to the class can help students regulate and rely on the structure and consistency of the class's new goal: to do things differently so students can focus on learning a little better.

Tier 2/Tier 3 for the "disruptive" students—in groups or individually. In addition to incorporating a couple of whole-class strategies, the teacher can further focus the issue by gathering more data. The following questions address key pieces that will help the teacher design effective interventions:

- Is there a common time or subject when the disruptions tend to happen?
- What are the "antecedents" that precipitate the disruptions for any individual students?
- Are students triggering one another, or are they operating off their individual impulses?

Once the teacher has more detailed information, she can implement some targeted strategies to support students' impulse control, such as the following:

- Schedule check-in time so students know when it is coming.
- Shorten the amount of time between brain breaks, then incrementally build students' stamina over time as they experience success. As students learn to trust that the teacher can meet their needs effectively, they should rely less on needing frequent breaks and start to trust that breaks will come. Thus, the number of breaks in a day should decrease over time, but the teacher can always add more back in should the need arise during more chaotic or stressful periods (e.g., around holiday breaks or testing times).
- Assign jobs and responsibilities during the tougher transition times or at any other time students are dysregulated.
- Provide predictable expectations that students can recite to the teacher at each transition (e.g., answering these questions: *What is my expectation of you? What will I see you doing during this time? What will you look like? What do I need to see from you at the end of this time? Can you show me what that will be like?*).
- Discuss the effect of their behaviors. Are the students even aware of the way their antsiness affects others?

Now let's move on to more targeted intervention possibilities for each of the five stakeholder groups: student, parent/caregiver, teacher, support staff, and leader.

Student: These are students who are struggling with regulation. Clearly, each one is going to need some additional support to regain focus, attention, and calm and to get back into the learning mode. The following are some possible steps to take:

• *Try a variety of brain tools.* This is a great opportunity to hypothesize what might work for individual students and see how effective different strategies are. Some students may give the teacher a clue with their interests, hobbies, or habits. For example, if Mandy loves horses, keeping a small horse figurine in her pocket could be all she needs to regulate. If Russ is interested in how machines work and constantly fiddles with objects, a felt pad overlaying his desk will ensure his fiddling is silent. The teacher should feel free to experiment, asking students how they feel about certain tools, trying them out, keeping the ones that work, and discarding the others. Every child is unique, so it's OK if something works for one student and is a train wreck for another.

• *Assign a study buddy.* Many students do well when that one other classmate is nearby—that fellow student who helps them settle in, get to work, understand the material, and focus. Of course, sometimes this backfires spectacularly—that's why this is detective work.

• *Assign specific jobs related to students' interests or the academic content.* The teacher could, for example, ask one student to tally the number of times she hears the number 4, tell another to put a checkmark next to all the sight words he hears in the next five minutes, assign another to be the scout who identifies students who are focused and on-task, and ask another to monitor the amount of wait time the teacher uses between asking a question and calling on a student to answer.

• *Identify an adult champion for each student.* This champion—an adult who is fully in that student's corner and committed to helping him or her be successful—could become a destination for a short brain-break walk when needed. A quick visit to a trusted adult in another setting is sometimes just what is needed to help with regulation, focus, and calming. Even if the champion is teaching, being in his or her presence could have a soothing effect on the student.

Parent/caregiver: How can the school partner with the families of the disruptive students and gain their support? One possibility would be inviting them to volunteer in class and provide an extra set of hands to the teacher. When they come in, they could observe their child in action and work with the teacher to identify and address the student's needs. If the parents aren't available during the school day, setting up a conference at an alternative time or location would work better. If the meeting is off-site, I recommend that at least two staff members attend. At this conference, it's essential to maintain a positive, strength-focused, solution-oriented mindset. Parents know their children very well and should have astute insights into when their kids are successful, how they regulate at home, and what doesn't work—powerful information to have. With this partnership, the teacher can better attune to each student's unmet needs, whether they're related to regulation, academics, or something else entirely.

Teacher: We can all empathize with this teacher. How can she make sure she's staying in *her* upstairs brain when her students are misbehaving, disrupting class, and challenging the success of everyone involved? Does she know which behaviors trigger her into an emotional reaction? If she doesn't have a toolbelt full of self-regulation strategies, now would be a good time to create one. Self-awareness is the first step toward a positive resolution. She's on a slippery slope, as her deficit view of her students is starting to take hold; indeed, she's beginning to fear the worst possible outcomes related to these behaviors. She could use some help shifting her mindset so she can see her students' potential, strengths, and successful moments.

Support staff: Once intervention plans are in place, the support staff needs to be apprised of this information and trained to ensure they use the same language in their interactions with students that is being used in the classroom. Consistency and predictability are crucial here: all staff members need to be up to speed on how best to support the teacher and the students who are at risk.

Leader: First, this leader should provide some support to the teacher; this work is too demanding and complex to do alone. Connecting her with a mentor or a teammate who can check in with her frequently would be a great start. These check-ins could take the form of simple status reports, reminders to practice self-care, problem-solving sessions, positive reinforcement, sessions for brainstorming management techniques, or even the offer of a shoulder to cry on. If a formal partnership isn't viable, the principal, assistant principal, counselor, or instructional assistants can make it a priority to visit the classroom to assist when necessary, give the teacher a break to engage in her own self-regulation activities, or observe students to help identify needs. If the teacher needs ideas and professional development on routines and classroom management, the leader should make it happen. The goal is for the teacher to feel supported, not judged; cared for, not dismissed. This is one of the core responsibilities of building administration.

Scenario #2 (Middle School): Struggles with Deacon's Mother

A teacher shares his situation:

> I'm frustrated with the parent of an 8th grade student who is refusing to give consent for services for her son, Deacon, who is acting out in school. Deacon's behavior has led to suspension, and even the superintendent is involved. Our conversations with his mother have gone nowhere.

It is so hard to feel as though parents aren't supporting the needs of their children, especially when the student would clearly benefit from support and can't get what he needs because of his parent's seeming stubbornness. We pour so much of our heart and soul into helping our students that we often react emotionally when we perceive that other people in these students' lives aren't living up to their end of the bargain.

What makes me think both student and parent require a regulation-based intervention? This situation screams out for regulation because all parties involved are in their downstairs brains. The student, Deacon, is having significant behavior issues, which signal regulation struggles; his mother is refusing to partner, which indicates that she goes downstairs when the school attempts to connect; the teacher is dysregulated because of his anger at the parent and frustration with the student; and the fact that the superintendent is involved indicates that the school leadership is also struggling with this scenario.

What additional information can we gather? Are there some unanswered questions here? You bet! Rather than throwing interventions at this student and his mother like darts in the dark, let's collect some more information that will help school personnel target their attention and support as effectively as possible. The following are some questions to start with. What other information would you like to gather?

- What, exactly, are the behaviors that are resulting in Deacon's suspensions? Are they unsafe for him, other students, adults, or all of the above?
- What is triggering the behaviors in the first place? Are they occurring in the same places at predictable times of day? With the same students or staff? After certain transitions or experiences?
- What is the parent's history of communication and interaction with the school?
- Are there any staff members who have connected with the parent?
- Are there any staff members who have connected with Deacon?
- What does "consent for services" mean? What services is the school proposing?
- Why is the superintendent involved? What has elevated this situation to the district level?

First and foremost, the teacher has to look at what he does have control over (how he can handle and address this situation) instead of focusing on the things he doesn't have control over (the parent's consent and the student's behavior). Many of us too easily get caught up in our frustrations and disappointments and lose sight of our opportunity to work with what we do have in positive ways.

Building Empathy and Exploring Deacon's Scenario from Five Perspectives

Now let's explore Deacon's scenario from the perspective of five stakeholders: the student, the parent/caregiver, the teacher, support staff, and the leader.

Student: Deacon is struggling. He's in 8th grade, and I can only imagine what his systems of meaning are by now. It appears that as the school pushes, he digs in harder, to the point that this situation has become a multifaceted power struggle, including his mom and the superintendent. It doesn't seem to be working: this is fast becoming a high-risk situation. How long will Deacon stick it out? He's sending a message that he's not OK, and the only strategy he has is to act out. I wonder when he last felt liked by the adults at school. When has he felt successful and worthwhile? How overwhelming must it be to live up to his reputation day in and day out? His behavior at school tells us that he may well be battling at home, too.

Parent/caregiver: Holy cow, is this mom overwhelmed. What goes through her head (and heart) when she is contacted by the school to be told of all that is not working with her son? I'm sure her systems of meaning about education are not positive. She's probably feeling like she's been backed into a corner, forced into the protective dance of defending her son, trying to justify that he's a good kid. Her experience with him could be completely different from the school's, and she may be trying to understand what has happened. Why do they think her son is so bad, so out of control, and so hopeless that he needs some special program?

Teacher: Deacon's teacher is wrestling with this situation, too. He truly believes that his student's needs outweigh his capacity to meet them. Thus, he has cultivated a belief in and reliance on outside services. If he can't help Deacon adequately, someone out there must be able to, right? Imagine coming to work every day knowing it's going to be a battle you're not equipped for. That's got to feel exhausting, defeating, demoralizing. Sadly, all the outside services in the world aren't going to fix the rupture that has occurred between the school and the home in this scenario. That will require some finessing by the adults in the equation.

Support staff: We don't know the extent to which any support staff members are involved, but because this is middle school, there are likely several other teachers, paraprofessionals, and other staff members who have interacted with Deacon. What have those been like? Do staff members walk on eggshells around Deacon, worried that he might blow? Do they reach out to his mom, too, or is that just one teacher's responsibility? There isn't anything in this scenario about other staff, but I would guess that other adults have a similar take on it.

Leader: This must be a significant issue if the superintendent is involved. Most school administrators prefer to handle their highest-profile situations in-house. Perhaps the school believes in an alternate placement for Deacon, supporting the teacher's perspective that outside services are warranted here. This is most likely an emotionally draining, frustrating experience for the leader—attempting to meet a tough student's needs, mediating between school and home, and trying to support the teacher.

Building a Plan to Support Deacon and His Family: Possible Interventions

In this section, I offer targeted intervention possibilities for each of the five stakeholders: student, parent/caregiver, teacher, support staff, and leader.

First things first. This is not a situation that any individual teacher, administrator, or counselor can handle solo. This is a perfect opportunity to convene the team, and I would guess that there have already been several team meetings to brainstorm strategies to support Deacon and all the adults in the picture. Those meetings may not have explored regulation-based interventions, though. Some possibilities follow.

Student: If Deacon's behaviors have escalated to the point that the superintendent is involved, that means it's a safety issue, and my guess is that Deacon is self-harming or harming others. If his recourse is to use his fists, he has two significant needs.

First, he needs a strategy to help him self-regulate when he begins to feel threatened, anxious, or unsafe. Standing up, walking away, counting to 10 backward, and getting a drink of water are all simple but effective strategies. If it is indeed his hands that are doing the damage (e.g., hitting, punching, or pushing), it might help him to stuff them into his pockets, to intentionally interlace his fingers together, or to grab his opposite shoulders. Physical motion such as this can help him keep his hands occupied while reminding his brain to stay online.

Second, Deacon could use a replacement strategy to demonstrate and communicate his fear, anger, or frustration instead of hurting others (or possibly himself). Perhaps he could learn a mantra, something to say when he's stressed, to cue himself and anyone around him: "I'm going to climb the ladder right now" or "I'm going to rise above this" can be helpful self-talk. It could even be as direct as "I have to bounce."

Whichever regulation and replacement strategies are selected—and Deacon is old enough to have some say here—the key is to teach them to Deacon, giving him multiple opportunities to practice them, refine them, and rehearse them in a safe environment, when he's in his upstairs brain. If Deacon's team can help him make his use of these strategies automatic, he'll be more likely to access them in moments of stress.

Parent/caregiver: Deacon's parent would likely benefit from an invitation to partner in this situation. The school personnel have their ideas and Deacon's mom has hers, but ultimately, they're all on the same team: team Deacon! How might the school reach out to this mother to engage in an open discussion and exploration of her perspective? At a time when Deacon is not in trouble for his dangerous behaviors, she could visit the school (or a school team could conduct a home visit, or everyone could meet at a neutral location) and just sit and talk. No mention of suspensions, expulsions, additional assessments, alternative placements, or Deacon's past behaviors—simply a conversation, preferably over a cup of coffee or some upstairs brain–fueling food like fresh veggies or fruit.

Teacher: This teacher, overwhelmed as he is, could use the team's emotional and strategic support. Sometimes just knowing that we're not in this alone and that we've got a team of concerned, supportive professionals in our corner is all we need to persist through tough times. It's also helpful to share the load. Does Deacon have a safe adult on staff? Can that person get more involved, perhaps teaching Deacon regulation and replacement strategies or serving as a regular contact with whom Deacon can check in daily? Also, does Deacon's teacher have positive self-talk strategies? Does he have ways to reactivate his upstairs brain in stressful times? Perhaps this is an avenue to explore.

Support staff: This scenario has provided a good opportunity to convene the staff (those who interact with Deacon or even the entire faculty) and engage in a discussion about the toxic effects of stress and trauma on the brain of developing youth. Surfacing lessons like

"It's not about you" can do wonders for everyone involved, helping staff members to calibrate their approaches in a strength-based, solution-oriented, collaborative manner.

Leader: Site administrators have the ultimate responsibility here: coordinating the supports that the team wants to put in place for Deacon, his mother, and the staff. That means inviting all the essential parties to the table, when everyone is regulated, to facilitate an open team-building discussion. If the principal is dysregulated because the situation has escalated to the superintendent level, taking a step back and attempting to see the scenario from a 30,000-foot altitude is in order. The principal needs to ask herself, "If this were a colleague at a neighboring building, what advice would I offer?"

Scenario #3 (High School): Reengaging Joey

Joey is a sophomore with a history of struggling in school. He is generally well liked by his fellow students, but not so much by the staff in the building. He tends to skip class, and when he is in class, he often attempts to distract others from the learning process. He isn't afraid to stand up to adults, and some adults in the building are afraid of Joey, so they let him get away with things to avoid confrontation. The parents are disengaged and tired of the school looking to them to solve their son's problems.

This is not atypical for high school, and I work with scenarios like this quite often. They center around the dilemma of when to reach out and provide *availability* to students as opposed to enforcing *accountability* because "by now students should know better." This also brings up the age-old question: who should be working harder at this point—the staff, the parents, or the student? There are two things I'd like us to keep in mind here: First, Joey might have muscles and facial hair and a deep voice *and* still be a kid. His brain is still growing and developing, and he needs both availability *and* accountability from his school. If he does indeed know better, he either isn't sure about how to do better or is lost in the path that he's on. Second, it's not a matter of who is working the hardest; it's about doing what we can to ensure Joey's success. We all share a responsibility for supporting each and every one of our students and one another.

What makes me think Joey requires a regulation-based intervention? Joey is clearly struggling in school, and he has a history of *not* being in a learning-ready state. The fact that he attempts to derail the learning process and recruit his classmates into his off-task behaviors and sometimes skips school altogether tells me that he has become a master of avoidance. Confronting his teachers appears to be a downstairs-brain, survival-mode response when he's not regulating, and things seem to be spiraling out of control from there.

What additional information can we gather? The following are some things I'm wondering about:

- What is Joey's status academically?
- The fact that Joey is liked by his peers tells me he has had some successes. What have those been?
- Is there a class Joey is more likely to attend more than others?
- Is there a teacher he has had success with?
- What is Joey's goal at this point? Is he interested in graduating? Does he have notions about going to college? Trade school? A vocational program? The military? Straight to work?
- When he skips class, where does he go? What does he do?
- Has he been in the same district since kindergarten, or has he moved around?

- Has he had discipline issues that have resulted in out-of-school suspension?
- How long has Joey's behavior followed this pattern?
- Have his disinterest and dysregulation been consistent over time, or have they recently increased?

Building Empathy and Exploring Joey's Scenario from Five Perspectives

Now let's explore Joey's scenario from the perspective of five stakeholders: the student, the parent/caregiver, the teacher, support staff, and the leader.

Student: Poor Joey. This little guy, who might be 6'4" and 220 pounds for all we know—and is still a kid, mind you—has been struggling for a long time, and no one has found a way to make things better for him. I am sure his systems of meaning are not great when it comes to school, and I am concerned about his self-concept. I am glad he is liked by his peers, but at what cost does that popularity come? I am worried about how he is managing his dysregulation and which coping devices he has accessed to manage his stress. I can only imagine all the untapped talent Joey has that has gotten lost in the way he is viewed at school.

Parent/caregiver: Joey's parents must have developed a serious case of stress because of their relationship and history with the school. If they have only heard what isn't working for their son, they must be exhausted and at a total loss as to how to communicate and make it better. I am wondering what Joey's home life is like. Has he endured adverse experiences that have added to his struggles at school? Have his behaviors caused significant strain in his relationship with his parents? Or is he thriving at home and just disconnected from school? The last thing the school wants is for these parents to give up on their son. I feel so sad for parents who are put in positions of helplessness and eventually become nonresponsive. I am curious about Joey's parents' education history and their overall systems of meaning about education, and how much of that has carried into their relationship with their son.

Teacher and support staff: How sad that this situation has reached the point that Joey is not liked by the staff of his school. How lonely for him, and how frustrating for the staff. I get it: when we work harder than our students and feel disrespected and underappreciated, we want to just give up and move on, hoping that the "problem" kids will figure it out someday. I understand feeling overwhelmed and exhausted by our many responsibilities and how easy it would be just to focus on the kids who seem to care about their education. I empathize—I do! But we just don't get to quit. Joey needs his teachers now more than ever, and his behavior isn't personal—it's survival-driven. Looking at this from a larger, collective perspective, this isn't about us—it's about a young boy who needs us. Joey isn't giving us a hard time; he is having a hard time. He is a great example of why we need to be a "we" in these efforts. We can't do this alone—our jobs are hard enough as it is. All the Joeys in our buildings need us.

Leader: I am sure that by this point, the leadership is tired of hearing staff complain about Joey. I am sure the school leaders have heard that they haven't been tough enough on Joey and the consequences they have tried just aren't working. Well, guess what? They aren't. And maybe it isn't the consequences that are the issue, but the leadership and staff's failure to engage Joey in the right ways. Maybe they need support in better understanding Joey and his needs rather than focusing on how he is asking for them to be met. Joey's success isn't solely the responsibility of the leadership, nor is his need to be accountable for his actions. Everyone should be a resource for Joey.

Building a Plan to Support Joey: Possible Classroom Interventions

Joey has a history with staff, his academic record is full of information, and he is growing and developing as a young person. It's time to call up the troops, circle the wagons, compile all the information, and gather input from as many sources as possible to support him. If there were ever a student crying out for teaming, it'd be Joey. All the key stakeholders need to get together and see what plans they can create to meet Joey's needs. Here are some ideas.

Student: Joey is the most important person in the room, so the intervention should start with him. The team needs to ask him for his perspective and truly listen. The adults involved need to figure out what makes Joey tick. What are his interests, his goals, and his hobbies? What does he want to do with his life? If focus and engagement are the issue because he's not regulating, that's the place to start. What brain tools, brain breaks, or other activities might help Joey attend to his learning? Does Joey have requests, ideas, or suggestions? Because attendance is an obvious prerequisite for learning and Joey is missing a lot of school, the team also needs to help him create a plan for coming to school, staying there, and connecting with someone who can help him regulate while he's there. Does he have a champion? A mentor? Is there a student mentoring program in place that pairs seniors with sophomores and juniors with freshmen to help usher underclassmen through the first two years of high school? Perhaps learning some regulation strategies together could help them both, and the partnership might address Joey's lack of motivation to attend school in the first place.

Parent/caregiver: How can the school transmit the message to Joey's parents that their son is awesome, capable, and full of potential, and that plenty of opportunities to succeed await him at school? They need to hear that—soon! School staff can engage them in a team meeting in which the topic *du jour* is the school's collective goal for Joey. Joey can and should be a part of this discussion. When school staff members shift the focus of their communications from deficits and problems to strengths and solutions, the parents are more likely to partner with them, engage regularly, and see them as allies as opposed to "those school people who complain about Joey all the time."

Teacher and support staff: Let's team this one. Whom has Joey been successful with? What has worked? How did learning look in that atmosphere? What kinds of interventions does Joey respond best to? What kinds of consistent structures, expectations, and plans can the team put in place? One of the biggest issues in secondary schools for kids who are struggling with regulation is that they must learn at least six different styles of teaching and classroom management along with the subject matter. That can be very overwhelming for students, and when they cannot assimilate into each unique environment, their behaviors can throw off their teachers, too. This scenario seems to involve power struggles between Joey and his teachers. What is happening to cause these conflicts? What can his teachers do to maintain a certain equilibrium and defuse tense situations? Perhaps it would be helpful for them to learn, practice, and master a couple of de-escalation strategies in addition to some self-regulation approaches to ensure that they, if not Joey, remain in their upstairs brains.

Leader: It's not surprising that after a while, interacting with Joey, assigning the same consequences over and over, responding to staff referrals, and spinning around the hamster wheel without making any notable progress can get tiring, exasperating, and emotionally draining. When leaders get emotional, others follow. Thus, school leaders have an incredibly important job: maintaining an emotionally dispassionate focus on the goal, process, and decisions that will keep everyone else in their upstairs brains, too. One way leaders can do this is to ask themselves the following key questions:

- What is your role?
- Whom are you working for?
- What is about to drive your behavior?

Leaders need to let the goals drive the approaches they choose. What is Joey's long-term goal? What does he envision for his future? No matter what he and his family have in store for him, the team's shared short-term goal is to get Joey back into the schoolhouse on a regular basis, in the learning mode, and reengaged in learning. He'll need skills in self-regulation *and* he'll need the adults in his life in their upstairs brains, reminding him that he's capable, competent, and full of potential. This is a marathon, and even though he's already in high school, there's still time to reconnect and achieve success. That's good, because it may take a while before everyone in this equation can trust one another, as their systems of meaning have been deeply affected by past interactions. They just need to take it one step at a time.

Conclusion

The ability to self-regulate is a prerequisite of learning. To be learning-ready, our students must be in their upstairs brains—regulated, self-aware, rational, and processing stimuli from multiple sources. Fortunately, this is a skill we can teach our students.

Regulation starts with us—the adults. When we are regulating, we are more likely to be under control, calm, reasonable, and teaching-ready. Simultaneously, we're less likely to access our own systems of meaning, get lost in behavior, or "flip our lids." Our regulation sets the tone for success in our buildings and classrooms. Taking care of our own wellness so we have the energy to regulate is a top priority. Modeling for our students the importance of regulating and being in our upstairs brain is the logical next step.

We can then assist our students in identifying tools and tricks that can help them achieve a learning-ready state. Naturally, this process must occur while both of you (adult and student) are in your upstairs brains. That way, you can discuss how it feels to be dysregulated, regulated, and teetering on the brink—and what might help your students get back "online." Together, you can explore different approaches, devices, and strategies to see which have the greatest positive effect, when they work best, and how to use them without causing undue disruptions to anyone else in the classroom. Remember, this is about problem solving and partnership. You've got this!

Conclusion: Not Perfect, and ... Enough

A while back, when I was walking on the beach between writing sessions, I came across the words "Not perfect, and ... enough" etched into the sand. Should I have been surprised to find such deep philosophical musings in the place where I find my greatest peace and psychological flow? As I read it I thought, *This is the perfect idea to end this book!* It sums it up just right. As professionals in the education and caregiving arenas, we work *hard*. The struggle is real, and the challenge to maintain a reasonable and healthy work-life balance can be overwhelming. Many of us fight this battle daily: when are our efforts good enough?

Compounding the issue is grief. I see grief as a powerful, prevalent influence in education right now. Grief from seasoned staff members who mourn what teaching used to be and who struggle with changes in expectations and student populations and behaviors. I see grief in new staff members who are struggling to accept a reality of teaching that is far different from what they fantasized it would be. And you know what? We have a right to grieve and to be not-OK. *And* we need to avoid getting stuck there and caught up in what was or what should have been.

I am here to remind us of the fact that we may not be perfect, and we are . . . enough. We need to see ourselves with the same potential that we attribute to our students. It's essential that we view one another—not 70 percent, but 100 percent of us—with the capabilities to be awesome. We are all working hard to achieve and provide the very best we can for those we work for and with. It is important that we do our best not only for ourselves but also for our students and families. It is also important that we set realistic goals and expectations for what that looks like.

Stress Is an Unfortunate Companion

All too often, I have seen students rip up papers because they weren't perfect, get stuck and not move forward because they fear failure, or become suicidal out of fear that they won't make a team or will lose their scholarship. At the same time, I have worked with families who fully believe that they can never get out of poverty, that their children are destined for prison, or that they have no hope of breaking cycles of violence and addiction.

How did we get to a place of such extremes? What is realistic, and how can we set expectations that result in success for each and every one of us? Although it is important to set a high bar, it is also essential to teach future adults about health and balance. We live in a country that values long work days, high stress, and overachievement—to the detriment of many. Sometimes those heightened expectations can immobilize us and result in our doing nothing. I fear our priorities have gotten a bit muddled.

Life is messy, and we can never fully avoid the mess. There is no bubble wrap to protect us from stress, fear, and pain. The mess is just a reality that comes with life, and we cannot let it be the thing that drives our bus. I know firsthand how easy it is to get overwhelmed by the mess. As I write this book, I am in the process of caring for my mom, who is dying from cancer. My mom is one of the strongest and smartest women I know. I am not sure if she will make it to see this book in print, and I appreciate every day for the time I get to spend with her. It is not easy, being a single mom of two children (one at college and one at home), caring for an ill parent who lives in a different state, managing two jobs, paying a mortgage, attempting to have a relationship, and . . . well, just living life. You know the drill. You may be managing similar messes. It isn't easy, to say the least.

We can easily fall into that trap of admiring our problems and getting lost in how hard things are. We can become easily overwhelmed by what we are not doing well, what we didn't get to, and what isn't working. That can weigh us down and get us on a path to nowhere good. When we do this, it makes it hard to see the beauty and the grace in every day. I am fully aware of the fact that as my stress level grows, so does the likelihood that the Eeyore-Pooh balance in my personality will get out of whack. Eeyore (the negative, downtrodden, pessimistic side) will emerge more prominently, while Pooh (the jovial, fun-loving, optimistic side) fades into the background. I'll focus on the negative or worry about things more, raising my stress levels. And stress is a horrible thing for us humans—it wreaks havoc on our minds and our bodies.

Can we avoid stress? Nope. Can we find ways to manage it more effectively? Yep.

What we are trying to do for our students and families living with trauma is not to provide a silver bullet that takes their stress away, but to help them find healthy ways to manage the stress. And practicing what we preach is not just good role-modeling; it's also a healthy way to live. We need to persevere despite adversity and give others that same skill. Resilience is powerful, and it is something we can foster in ourselves and those around us.

So, how can we commit to a realistic goal, and what does it really look like to have a healthy work-life balance? I consult with hard-working, dedicated teachers and administrators all the time, and often my interventions include this fundamental two-part prescription:

1. Go home. Come in at a reasonable hour at least twice a week and leave at a reasonable hour at least twice a week. Trust me, the work will still be there.

2. Share the load. Help your teammates and ask them to help you, so everyone—not just a few dedicated warriors—can take on the burden together.

It's also important to remember that life is bigger than us! You already know this, but it's worth repeating. Rather than getting mired in the ruts and negativity, let's take the reins and start a movement: let's give ourselves and one another boundless grace. If we truly want a healthy work-life balance, grace could well be the key.

I love to read stories about those who choose to help others. They warm my heart and remind me of the good in this world. We need to find ways to share these stories and encourage others to promote this good. Grace is a big part of this, and it can be given in so many ways: simply saying "thank you," buying coffee for the person behind us in line, giving a student an extra day to finish a paper, shoveling the neighbor's driveway after a heavy snowfall, bringing a hot meal to a friend who is ill, giving a high-five to a stranger, sending a note to someone in the mail, forgiving a fault of another, letting the other driver merge ahead of you in traffic, and so many more. When is the last time you offered grace to another? How did it feel? When we appreciate others and offer grace, our sense of self becomes better and brighter.

"Promise me you'll always remember: You're braver than you believe, and stronger than you seem, and smarter than you think."
                        —Winnie the Pooh, to his pal Christopher Robin

My colleague and dear friend Anna Rowe came across this quote from a *Winnie the Pooh* video. It resonated with me so strongly. Isn't this the message we want our students leaving us with? That their sense of self and resilience will help them enter their future stronger, braver, and wiser?

A Quick Summary

What I've shared with you and asked of you in this book is fairly straightforward. It all starts with self-awareness and self-care. Because we know childhood trauma is real and prevalent, and we really don't know which of our students have experienced an adverse event, it's our obligation to create a culture of safety—a safe, consistent, and predictable nest—for every child under our care. Although we cannot stop trauma from happening, we can shape the setting in which our young people find themselves every day. Part of establishing this nest is being aware of our systems of meaning, knowing that past experiences, tales, social media, and other sources influence the way we think and act in certain circumstances. They affect what we believe and the paths we choose to follow. Again, this is something over which we can be in complete control.

Then, very importantly, we turn our eye toward our students. Becoming mindful that every behavior is an expression of an unmet need, we can identify exactly what our students need and then begin to implement a plan to address it. By using the new three *R*s as a lens and a framework, we can support our students in specific, intentional, proactive, and positive ways. I hope that the scenarios I've presented and the strategies I've suggested from all angles—as we circle the wagons around each kid in our nest—have helped bring this approach to life for you.

A Brain-Friendly Self-Care Challenge

Although we may not be perfect, we are enough. The need for our own mind-body-spirit health is crucial in helping us to achieve and maintain that balance. Our own resilience and perseverance can be a powerful role model to those we serve. So, by way of a conclusion, I'd like to reissue a self-care challenge, modified from the version first proposed in *Fostering Resilient Learners*. I am asking you to adopt nine essential behaviors that will help your brain become healthier, stronger, and more responsive—leading to that ultimate work-life balance. Try these for 28 days (and beyond):

1. **Drink plenty of water.** Thirsty brains can't teach, and thirsty brains can't learn. So when you're thirsty, and even if you think you're not, have some more water.

2. **Eat upstairs-brain food.** Food is our fuel, so let's put high-octane meals and snacks into our bodies. Try beans, whole grains, poultry and fish, nuts, and plenty of fruits and veggies.

3. **Exercise.** Yes, you have time, if you prioritize it. Try to incorporate some physical activity for 40 minutes three times a week, or 30 minutes five times a week.

4. **Sleep.** That's right, we need to be rested to operate at full capacity. Snooze deeply for eight hours every night for 28 days and see how your body responds.

5. Challenge yourself. Force your brain to make new connections by doing something different, taking a risk, trying something you've never done before.

6. Work as a team. By combining forces, sharing the workload, and collaborating, you can maximize your efficiency and build social networks, too.

7. Breathe. Just breathe. As I wrote in *Fostering Resilient Learners,* "When in doubt, shut your mouth and take a breath." Feel free to practice mindfulness, do yoga, meditate . . . just breathe.

8. Limit screen time. Devices run our lives—when we let them. Power up by powering down: designate a no-device window, turn off the TV, read a real book, play a game, take a walk. See if you can limit your recreational screen time to less than two hours per day.

9. Show your gratitude. We have so much to be thankful for, even if it's temporarily hidden. Every day, acknowledge something or someone in an intentional way.

In the online study guide that pairs with this book (available at http://www.ascd.org/publications/books/119027/chapters/An-ASCD -Study-Guide-for-Relationship,-Responsibility,-and Regulation .aspx), Pete and I put together a brain health self-care challenge chart for you and your team to complete. Use this chart and repeat for four weeks. At the end of 28 days, engage in some deep self-reflection about your journey, your goals, and your progress. What worked for you? What do you need to change? Which of the nine brain-healthy behaviors did you find the easiest to incorporate? Which were more difficult? How is your energy? Your attention? Your endurance? Did this 28-day challenge affect your work? Your relationships? At what level is your *powerometer* (a term Pete uses to describe one's energy level, strength, attitude, and overall zest for life and its many challenges)? Invite your students and families to participate as well. Let's see how you do!

If you're more successful keeping track of your efforts and progress through a journal, with a partner or group, or vlogging, that's fine, too! As long as you are strategic and deliberate about your steps and have a way to gauge the effect they are having on your life, great. Take time each day to take stock of how things are going and to appreciate yourself, your mind, your body, and your spirit. Give yourself the grace and the care that you deserve. You will be better for others when you make time to take care of yourself.

A Closing Thought

Thank you. No matter what your role is, know that it's important in the life of a child. Or two. Or 200. Or 200,000! The young people in our lives, in our society, in our world depend on us—the caring, safe, predictable, consistent adults—to help them make sense of this journey and become better equipped to handle it on their own. That is a significant responsibility! So we thank you—for taking time to read this book, for reflecting deeply on your own beliefs and practices, for dedicating your energy and heart to our kids, and for remaining steadfast in your mission.

Now: go be awesome!

Bibliography

Balfanz, R., Byrnes, V., & Fox, J. (2015). Sent home and put off track: The antecedents, disproportionalities, and consequences of being suspended in the 9th grade.
In D. J. Losen (Ed.), *Closing the school discipline gap: Equitable remedies for excessive
exclusion*. New York: Teachers College Press.

Baum, L. (1900). *The wonderful wizard of Oz*. Chicago: George M. Hill Co.

Blaustein, M., & Kinniburgh, K. (2010). *Treating traumatic stress in children and adolescents: How to foster resilience through attachment, self-regulation, and competency*.
New York: Guilford Press.

Brown, J. (2008). *Educating the whole child*. Alexandria, VA: ASCD.

Check & Connect information page. (n.d.). Check & Connect Student Engagement
Intervention, Institute on Community Integration, University of Minnesota.
Retrieved from http://checkandconnect.umn.edu/research/default.html

Clear, J. (n.d.). Rome wasn't built in a day, but they were laying bricks every hour
[Blog post]. *James Clear*. Retrieved from https://jamesclear.com/lay-a-brick

Coleman, J. S., Campbell, E. Q., Hobson, C. J., McPartland, J., Mood, A. M.,
Weinfeld, F. D., et al. (1966). *Equality of educational opportunity*. Washington, DC:
National Center for Educational Statistics. Retrieved from https://files.eric.ed.gov
/fulltext/ED012275.pdf

Dweck, C. (2006). *Mindset: The new psychology of success*. New York: Ballantine Books.

Felitti, V. J., Anda, R. F., Nordenberg, D., Williamson, D. F., Spitz, A. M., Edwards, V.,
et al. (1998). Relationship of childhood abuse and household dysfunction to
many of the leading causes of death in adults: The adverse childhood experiences
(ACE) study. *American Journal of Preventive Medicine, 14*(4), 245–258.

Good Morning America. (2017). Teacher has personalized handshakes with every
single one of his students [Video]. Retrieved from https://www.youtube.com
/watch?v=I0jgcyfC2r8

Greene, R. (2008). *Lost at school: Why our kids with behavioral challenges are falling
through the cracks and how we can help them*. New York: Scribner.

Hall, P. (2011). *Lead on! Motivational lessons for school leaders*. Larchmont, NY:
Eye On Education.

Hoerr, T. (2013). *Fostering grit: How do I prepare my students for the real world?* (ASCD Arias). Alexandria, VA: ASCD.

Losen, D. J., Ee, J., Hodson, C., & Martinez, T. (2015). Disturbing inequities: Exploring the relationship between racial disparities in special education identification and discipline. In D. J. Losen (Ed.), *Closing the school discipline gap: Equitable remedies for excessive exclusion.* New York: Teachers College Press.

Marvin, R., Cooper, G., Hoffman, K., & Powell, B. (2002). The Circle of Security project: Attachment-based intervention with caregiver–pre-school child dyads. *Attachment & Human Development, 4*(1), 107–124.

Maslow, A. H. (1943). A theory of human motivation. *Psychological Review, 50,* 370–396.

Medina, J. (2008). *Brain rules: 12 principles for surviving and thriving at work, home, and school.* Seattle: Pear Press.

Milne, A. A. (1926). *Winnie-the-Pooh.* London: Methuen.

National Commission on Excellence in Education. (1983, April). *A nation at risk: The imperative for educational reform.* Washington, DC: Author. Retrieved from https://www2.ed.gov/pubs/NatAtRisk/index.html.

Pierson, R. (2013). *Every kid needs a champion* [Video]. TED Talks Education. Retrieved from https://www.ted.com/talks/rita_pierson_every_kid_needs_a_champion

Shollenberger, T. (2015). Racial disparities in school suspension and subsequent outcomes: Evidence from the National Longitudinal Survey of Youth. In D. J. Losen (Ed.), *Closing the school discipline gap: Equitable remedies for excessive exclusion* (pp. 31–43). New York: Teachers College Press.

Siegel D. J. (2003). An interpersonal neurobiology of psychotherapy: The developing mind and the resolution of trauma. In M. Solomon & D. J. Siegel (Eds.), *Healing trauma: Attachment, mind, body, and brain.* (pp. 1–56). New York: Norton.

Siegel, D. (2017). *Dr. Dan Siegel's hand model of the brain* [Video]. Retrieved from https://www.youtube.com/watch?v=f-m2YcdMdFw

Skiba, R. J. (2015). Interventions to address racial/ethnic disparities in school discipline: Can systems reform be race-neutral? In R. Bangs & L. E. Davis (Eds.), *Race and social problems* (pp. 107–124). New York: Springer.

Souers, K., & Hall, P. (2016). *Fostering resilient learners: Strategies for creating a trauma-sensitive classroom.* Alexandria, VA: ASCD.

Index

Note: Page references followed by an italicized *f* indicate information contained in figures.

About the Authors

 **Kristin Van Marter Souers** is a licensed mental health counselor in the state of Washington. Kristin has a Master of Arts degree in counseling psychology from Gonzaga University and a Bachelor of Science degree from Santa Clara University. Kristin is considered an expert in understanding the impact of trauma on individuals and families. She has provided countless professional development trainings and consultations with schools, districts, and community-serving agencies throughout the United States and is dedicated to supporting and sustaining the development of trauma-invested practices. She has written numerous articles and is the lead author of *Fostering Resilient Learners* (ASCD, 2016). She can be reached at ksouers@comcast.net.

 **Pete Hall** currently serves as a speaker, an author, and a professional development agent for schools and districts around the globe. A former teacher and veteran school principal, Pete is the author of more than a dozen articles on school leadership and author or coauthor of seven books, including *Building Teachers' Capacity for Success* (ASCD, 2008), *Teach, Reflect, Learn* (ASCD, 2015), *The Principal Influence* (ASCD, 2015), *Fostering Resilient Learners* (ASCD, 2016), and *Creating a Culture of Reflective Practice* (ASCD, 2017). In addition to his leadership work, Pete passionately advocates for the establishment of

trauma-invested learning environments, education that addresses the whole child, and the relentless quest for continuous improvement. He can be reached at petehall@educationhall.com.

Learn more about the work Kristin and Pete are doing by visiting their website: www.fosteringresilientlearners.org.

Related ASCD Resources

At the time of publication, the following resources were available (ASCD stock numbers appear in parentheses).

Print Products

Better Than Carrots or Sticks: Restorative Practices for Positive Classroom Management by Dominique Smith, Douglas B. Fisher, and Nancy E. Frey (#116005)

Discipline with Dignity, 4th edition: How to Build Responsibility, Relationships, and Respect in Your Classroom by Richard L. Curwin, Allen N. Mendler, and Brian D. Mendler (#118018)

Engaging Students with Poverty in Mind: Practical Strategies for Raising Achievement by Eric P. Jensen (#113001)

Even on Your Worst Day, You Can Be a Student's Best Hope by Manny Scott (#117077)

Fostering Resilient Learners: Strategies for Creating a Trauma-Sensitive Classroom by Kristin Souers with Pete Hall (#116014)

Teaching to Strengths: Supporting Students Living with Trauma, Violence, and Chronic Stress by Debbie Zacarian, Lourdes Alvarez-Ortiz, and Judie Haynes (#117035)

For up-to-date information about ASCD resources, go to **www.ascd.org**. You can search the complete archives of Educational Leadership at **www.ascd.org/el**.

PD Online

Classroom Management: Building Effective Relationships, 2nd Edition (#PD11OC104M)

Classroom Management: Managing Challenging Behavior, 2nd Edition (#PD14OC015)

An Introduction to the Whole Child (#PD13OC009M)

ASCD myTeachSource®

Download resources from a professional learning platform with hundreds of research-based best practices and tools for your classroom at http://myteachsource.ascd.org/.

For more information, send an e-mail to member@ascd.org; call 1-800-933-2723 or 703-578-9600; send a fax to 703-575-5400; or write to Information Services, ASCD, 1703 N. Beauregard St., Alexandria, VA 22311-1714 USA.

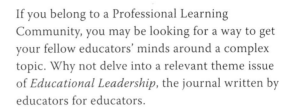

WHOLE CHILD
TENETS

1 HEALTHY
Each student enters school healthy and learns about and practices a healthy lifestyle.

2 SAFE
Each student learns in an environment that is physically and emotionally safe for students and adults.

3 ENGAGED
Each student is actively engaged in learning and is connected to the school and broader community.

4 SUPPORTED
Each student has access to personalized learning and is supported by qualified, caring adults.

5 CHALLENGED
Each student is challenged academically and prepared for success in college or further study and for employment and participation in a global environment.

THE **WHOLE CHILD**

The ASCD Whole Child approach is an effort to transition from a focus on narrowly defined academic achievement to one that promotes the long-term development and success of all children. Through this approach, ASCD supports educators, families, community members, and policymakers as they move from a vision about educating the whole child to sustainable, collaborative actions.

Relationship, Responsibility, and Regulation relates to the **healthy**, **safe**, **engaged**, **supported**, and **challenged** tenets. *For more about the ASCD Whole Child approach, visit* **www.ascd.org/wholechild.**

LEARN. TEACH. LEAD.